Me vs Me, You vs You

A Poetic Journey Through Feeling Towards Healing

DL Powers

Content Warning

Me vs. Me, You vs. You is a collection of poetry and prose that takes a deep dive into my self healing journey. While the path towards light and self love is powerful, there are moments in which darker topics are addressed and mentioned. I want to be sure my readers are aware of what they're diving into. If you have triggers, please be sure to take this list into consideration.

Your mental health matters.

This collection contains references regarding: depression and anxiety, terminal illness (specifically related to early onset Alzheimer's disease), grief, toxic relationships and subtle mentions of various forms of abuse.

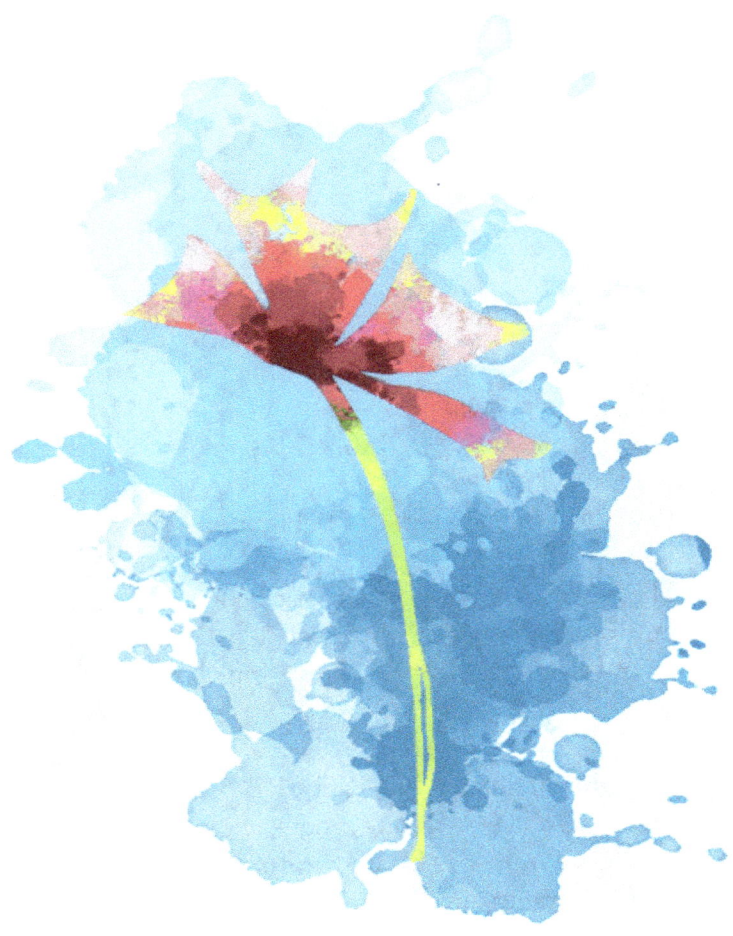

Me vs. Me, You vs. You
A Poetic Journey Through Feeling Towards Healing
by DL Powers
Copyright © 2024 by Flower Press Publications

The artwork on the front and back covers, along with page 62 ('*Mirror Mirror*'), are original paintings by Lynn Koski (@lynnkoski_art). All other interior graphics are paid stock images from Canva.com or Microsoft Word 2010.

All rights reserved. No part of this book may be reproduced or transmitted in any form or by any means, electronic or mechanical, including photocopying, recording, or by any information storage and retrieval system, without written permission from the author, except for the inclusion of brief quotations in a review.

This collection of poetry is a work of fiction. Unless otherwise indicated, any names, characters, places, events, and incidents in this book are either the product of the author's imagination or adapted and used in a fictitious manner. Any resemblance to actual persons, living or dead, or actual events is purely coincidental.

ISBN: 9798324213497
Printed in the United States

Table of Contents

PREFACE 9

PART I: THE INEXPLICABLE 11
    To The Ones Who Suffer in Silence 12
    Strong 15
    Box Thinkin' 16
    Suspended 17
    Floating, Floating 19
    Human Frailty 20
    Rivers Run On 21
    Paradox 23
    Reality 24
    Silenced 27
    Homo sapiens 28
    Typical 29
    Boys 31
    Passion 34
    Duplicity of Love 35
    Open The Door 36
    Intangible 37
    Uncovered 38
    Blue Jeans and Black Shirt 39
    A Single String 40
    Screen Doors 41
    Telephone Lines 43
    Touch 45
    Soñando Contigo 46
    Dreaming of You 47
    Sin to Love You 48
    Anguish 51
    Self 52
    Nothing is Something 53
    Made of Glass 55
    Soft Heart 57

PART II: THE BATTLE 59
    Pieces 60
    Mirror Mirror 62
    Nightmare 63
    Museum of My Identity 65
    Intertwined 67
    Temptation 69
    Roots 71

'Round and 'Round	72
Shadow	73
Lost	74
Out of the Gray	75
Wicked Sea	76
Dirty Dishes	78
In Between	79
Uneasy	80
Saving Smile	82
The Boogeyman	83
Yin and Yang	84
Drip Drip	85
Red Lines	86
Labyrinth of Life	87
Warrior	89
Sink	90
Reflection	92
Left Right Left	93
The Battle	95
The Demon Dance	97
Burn Away	99
Fire of Truth	101
The Yuck	102
Split	103
Pendulum	104
Sharp Edges	105
Yet it Shines	106
Haunting	107
Little Wound	108
Life	112
Chameleon	113
Protect	114
Trapped	115
Finding Myself	117
Grace	118
Are You Ready	119
Carried Away	120
Rage and Hope	121
Inescapable	122
Last Star	124
The Monster Within	125
Weapons	126
Keep Fightin'	127
Float Through the Storm with Me	129
Brown Eyes	130
The Thaw	131

PART III: THE HEALING 133

What If You Didn't Know the Sun?... 134
Invisible Child 136
Humanity 138
Seas of Life 140
Journey... 142
Love... 143
Bucket Full of Tears... 144
Age Demented 146
Extraordinary 149
Swept Away 150
Molded Clay 151
Clouds 152
Soaked Through... 153
Fear or Courage 154
Make a Splash.. 155
Ignited by the Light... 157
Beautiful Child... 158
Mother... 159
Baby Breath 160
Skeleton Key... 161
Fire Crackling Rose.. 162
The Light 163
As I Wander, I Wonder.. 164
What's Your Sunshine? 165
Nature's Music... 166
Fire, Water, Wind, and Earth 167
Game of Chess 168
Insignificant Significance 169
Creation is Quiet 170
Shadows.. 171
Walk Into Your Joy 173
I Am Not My Darkness 175
Rise Like the Sun 176
Resilience 177
Wish for You... 178
Pockets of Love 179
The Final Frontier.. 180
Me vs. Me 181

ACKNOWLEDGEMENTS... 185

INSPIRED BY... 187

Preface

I put this collection together as part of my healing journey. Part I: *The Inexplicable*, Part II: *The Battle*, Part III: *The Healing*. When I began writing, this distinction didn't seem significant. I doubted anyone would be curious about why I created it. Then I realized it matters because intent matters. But even more important is my hope that it evokes human feeling in you. From the heart-wrenching all the way through jubilation. When put out into the universe, may someone, someday, somehow find it, relate to it, and not feel so alone. My hope is that it provides you with the courage to push forward in *your* healing journey. That you would perhaps be inspired to explore *your* inner world and question with curiosity why you feel the way you do. Imagine if you will, my hand clasping yours and together we go diving, jumping, climbing, crawling if we must, into the world of mixed emotions. That we would go on a journey of healing despair, emptiness, and helplessness and leave empowered and inspired to explore our inner worlds. To question with curiosity, and ultimately leave you empowered to seek out your own healing. I'd love to hear about your experience, so you and I both don't feel so alone and can be better together. Therefore, I invite you to embark on this journey with me of inner feeling and inner healing. Healing is done in the quiet of our hearts. Have you also noticed growth is quiet? Heal and grow and let the feelings flow.

Part I: The Inexplicable

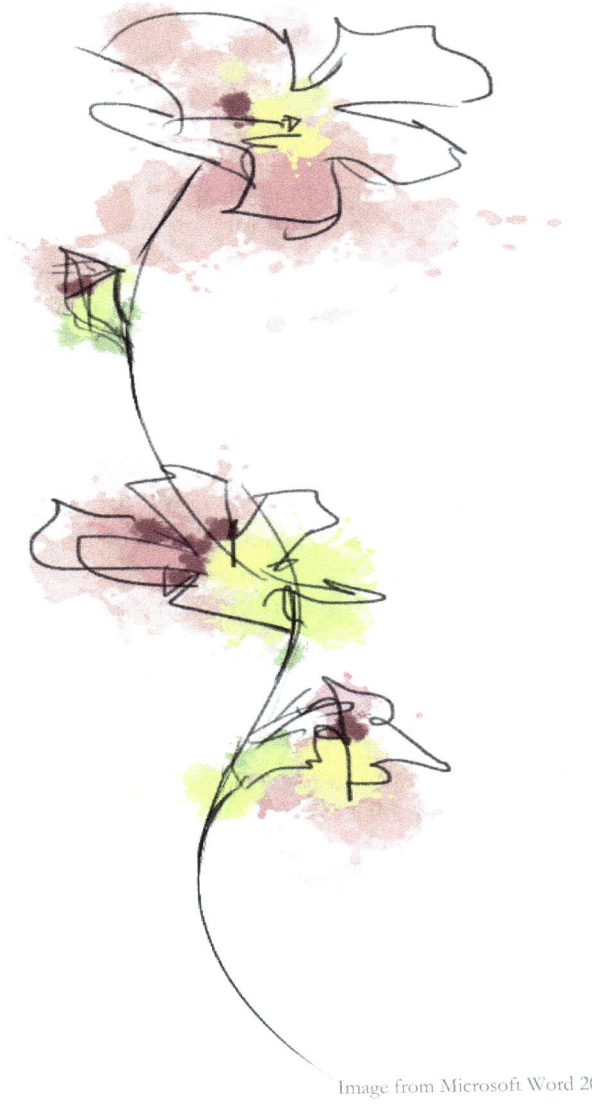

Image from Microsoft Word 2010

To The Ones Who Suffer in Silence

To the ones who suffer in silence,

> who bear the brunt of pain alone.

Do you ever feel like you have a superpower that you want all to behold?

> Yet you hold it in

hoping someone will secretly discover your unique gift.

Saving you from the weight and silence
and your loved ones from pain and anguish.

> Because the truth hurts so much
> you choose to keep it bottled inside
> like a sad and angry ghost.

Never letting anyone get too close.

> Like a genie in a bottle but your body is where the genie lies contained.

You allow the ghosts to run and hide and bury themselves in vain.

> You allow them to hide within your protective cover to shield others from feeling its burden and plunder.

Fearful that if this genie gets out,
it will tear through hearts
and rip your and their lives apart.

Secretly you hope if your genie would grant you one wish,
> it would be that your superpower allows you to physically touch someone, and they would just feel it all in a kind of healing transcendence.

Then they would feel and reveal a source of their own power waiting and ready to heal.

> You could turn this source of immense emotion and flip it on its head to be delivered through you like a magic potion.

A potion that's main ingredient is, hope, to help others cope and conquer.

Your superpower's intensity is so grand that it can turn the lethargic negativity into golden electricity.

> Yet, you sit and take it blow after blow, not really certain of which path to go. You stumble along hour after hour not letting others know of your genie's power.

Because if you told you know they wouldn't understand.

Like this,
at least they still have your helping hand.

Not using words to express your love for them. Let your actions speak of your benevolence and good intentions.

> You've given of yourself so selflessly. I'm so sorry you feel you must hold it under lock and key.

You don't deserve the hand dealt to you. You deserve to flourish light and free, ever so effervescent and abundantly.

> I'm here to share that it *doesn't* have to be left there. Left to die inside with you like so many of the others muddled in the quagmire of despair.

What would happen if you let it out? Would your pain cause the world to stop? Or would it help others and ease theirs? Releasing the shame and thought that you and they are the ones to blame?

> I don't pretend to know the answers for you, but at least we can share and help each other get through.

It's okay to allow the power to stay within the realms of your physical vessel.

> Be patient with yourself.

For when you are tired of the wrestle
> and are ready to let it go, it CAN fly free, carried by the breeze gently and with ease.

Flying far, far away releasing you of discontent and disease. Until then, I'm here to help let it flow, lightening the burden by giving love, hope, and support a chance to grow.

Strong

The strong one.
I think I need to be strong, which means not showing any weakness. I need not share my sadness with others, why burden them with my meekness?

I have always been viewed as strong, but deep down I know, I'm not the way others perceive.

I'm strong in my own way, in my ability to cry and hurt and bleed all over myself and then pick that all up, tuck it away, and move forward for my family.

I'm sorry when I'm not nice, or friendly, or proper or happy. I'm using all the energy I must just to push forward and stay standing.

Box Thinkin'

Think outside of the box, that's what we are taught from the age of three we begin to think for ourselves because that's the way we are brought up to be.

> Challenge your teachers, challenge yourself, challenge your country, but above all else...
>
> I challenge you to think outside of the country that has given you this "freedom" of thought.
>
> Outside you begin to see and ask, are we really thinking for ourselves or conditioned by the injected ideas and ideals given to us from the past, when we were just children?

You see from the inside one can't see beyond the red, white and blue. One needs to get out to really be free. Don't get me wrong, I love my country, the home of the "free."

I only ask thee to think outside of the box because you are in a land where you can, and this is such a luxury. Because on the contrary, once you think outside, you may end up appreciating and challenging aspects of your home even more. Thankful for those stars on the flag that shine so bright, representative of those dreamers who have given their lives, believing so strongly that they gave the ultimate sacrifice, so that the "US" can be better. They represent a beacon of possibility and hope to explore.

Suspended

So suspended am I
      in time and emotion.

Like a lone astronaut floating outside of their rocket looking down

      upon earth.   Suspended   in   space

in   awe   of   the   magnificence.

Light and free, every muscle at ease.

Yet all ALONE

      and not really
      sure how
      to get back
      down.

A heightened state of time in life where everything seems unreal.

But it is;

      just not like every other day.

It does not make the feelings less and on the contrary more!
      These moments don't come as often as the rest, making them
      seem invalid and ridiculous.

A ridiculous dramatization that makes the movies look like child's play.

The movies aren't real, but these moments stay.

Moments of love, lust, grief and hate

waiting for us to deliberate.

Floating, Floating

What is time and space?
We fill it. Or is it filled
for us?

We take up space.

What do we do with the space we fill?

What if space were unlimited as well as time?

Would we still appreciate life in the same way?

We grow, we shift, we form, we follow.

Love and pain exist to balance that
which is hollow.

Void of life and feeling and emotion.

Emotion is but a human blessing and a curse, as it tells us if
something is right or wrong.

It's part of humanity's song.

Human Frailty

We are so fragile, the humans that we are. One slit of the wrist and all the chances for a full life are gone.

One wrong word and humiliation and rejection trample us. One small mistake is never forgotten.

Fragile in mind, heart, character, and spirit. That's why our lives are so vulnerable and dramatic. It's why each day is worth living. Because at any one second it could all slip away.

Image from Microsoft Word 2010

Rivers Run On

The rivers run,
      the rivers of poisoned tears
           streaming from the windows to my soul.
                The current flows
                      blood red, symbolic
                            of heart-pumping purity.

But it turns into tar further downstream,
      tarnished from the hole
           you punctured,
           so easily,

      through my accepting and
unprotected heart.
But the rivers still flow,
  so strongly you can hear them,
        listen….
           can't you?

                        Along these rivers'
            lonely paths they cross.
            The poisonous tears intertwine with purity,
    and it becomes the essence of my being.

An explosion where soul and heart meet,
      the two sad rivers cancel each other out.
           A negative and a negative
                create a positive.

            This is when the intensity of my sentiments
are overwhelming and almost kill me with emotion.

The exhilaration and lust for life march on
      and it gives me hope.

        I wait patiently on those dark days
           for my rivers of the worst to cross

and provide me with the best.

    To know true happiness, we must also feel
the balance of true sadness.

My rivers rage on,
    and if you dare,
        jump in and take a ride
            through the rapids with self-care.

        You better hold on tight
      through these levels of complexity,
    and prepare yourself for utter darkness
and sheer ecstasy.

Paradox

        A walking paradox. A hypocrite in the most
        polarizing of ways.

The saying,
do what I say,
not what I do,
holds true.

        I try to stay in control
        to not be flung
        like a rag doll.

Side to side,
up and down
and all-around.

        But I lose myself
        sometimes forgetting
        which way is up.

        I need to bottle it up
        and hold a tight grip.

If I loosen it overboard,
I'll be thrown,
thrown from the ship.

        I am full of shit. I say I
        want one thing one
        moment, and I really
        mean it at the time,

but then I also really mean it
when I change my mind.

Reality

I realize the point is
I need to come to terms with the abuse.
I don't have an excuse
to continue to cope with what happened
to me or my precious family in ways
that are despicable and unthinkable
for a girl so lucky and smart as me.

What I once believed and
identified as my reality
is no more.
What I thought was real
is now surreal.
It makes me question
all from the past and
what shaped me into me.

Does that mean I'm made from lies?
I can pray all day,
but that won't take it away.

I accept that it likely happened.
I accept the damage.
But it's easier to pretend it didn't.

I'm supposed to turn it around and
frame it into something
positive and productive.
But it's seductive,
alluring….
And that won't stop it from
following my shadow.

Like a gift of coal wrapped in
a perfect box with a shiny bow,
but the gift is still dirty
and cold and heavy to carry.

Sometimes shit is shit
and there's no way to remove the stink
no matter how you wrap it up.
I should take that back,
the betrayal is real,
the empty is real, and
that will forever remain.

I live with it,
but I run
hoping to stay one step ahead,
not looking inside
to see what it reveals.

Sometimes I'm seduced
by its cunning pull.
Looking to hide,
searching for a place to escape
where it won't find my shadow's shape.

But I am only human,
and I grow tired and weary,
it knows nothing of
growing tired or worn down.
It eventually catches up to me
and on those days,
I fake pleasant and cheery.

On those days
I find it difficult to
keep it all together and balanced,
one false move and everything
feels as though it will come
crashing down and shatter.

So, I feed the demons
by sacrificing bits of myself,
so they are appeased and pleased
to have a little taste of me.

At least my coping is balanced with a mix of tactics.
Which is faulty logic and a use of nonsensical antics.
But it works.

I'm not supposed to let it define me
or so I have learned.
I won't.

But the split is something powerful.
We can't hide from ourselves;
we can't outrun our very own shadows.

Now that…….

That,

I know,

is real.

Silenced

She sits in the corner quietly
but not content.
She sits waiting to be heard,
but doesn't have the voice to speak
nor the content.

Hush little baby, don't you cry,
tomorrow's another day
to give it another try.
She tries again
but isn't taken seriously.

Her voice weakens and gets buried.
Maybe no one wants to hear
what she has to say?
Her cries and screams fall on deaf ears,
her tears aren't enough
and now it's become her worst fear.

She can't stand up,
she doesn't know how,
the ways she knows
aren't getting the message out!

She tells him she will let them know.
He twists and turns her words so that
she's the bad guy now.

With nowhere to turn
and no power to be heard,
it sits in her heart and hopelessly burns.

The power he maintains.
Silenced, she remains.

Homo sapiens

Why must we be so selfish?
Is that the defining factor
which allowed our species to survive?
It will likely also be the means to our demise.

Like the sun we can give off so much energy
and think everything revolves around us.

From a distance the sun is so beautiful.
But if we stare or bask below its outstretched rays for too long, we get burned by its blaze.

Like how we peer down at ants in their rank and file.
I wonder if someone is looking down at us just the same?

Maybe much like I described the sun,
they think that of us?

With our energy and capacity for love and joy
they would feel encouraged with a heart full of hope.

If they stare too long or get too close though,
I bet they see the ugly too.
Ants move to and fro with purpose, doing their jobs.
They are predictable.
We aren't.

We aren't because of this capacity
for love and hate and feeling.
If "they" look down at us homo sapiens long enough,
my wish is that they will see
the beauty more than the ugly.

What do you think?

Typical

I met a man the other day, sort of like three others I met.

His first question was:

1. "What is your name?"

"Jane," I replied.

Question number two:

2. "Are you married?"

"No," said I.

Question number three:

3. "Are you in love?"

"No," once again.

Question number four:

4. "Have you ever been?"

"Yes," I replied.

Question number five:

5. "Did he break your heart and make you cry?"

"Of course," said I.

"He doesn't know what he left behind," said the guy.

Question number six:

6. "Do you want to be married?"

"Right now, no, why?" I asked?

"Because you have to, you need to be with someone and put yourself in love."

"You can't just put yourself in love," I explained. He said, "Sure, you can, it's not hard if you try."

I replied back, "Sorry man,
when I marry it will take time
and be forever
until I die."

Question number 7:

7. "So, when do you plan to find your match?" he had to ask.

"Hey man, it's not something
I decide at the drop of a hat.
Why such questions so personal right off the bat?
What is your name anyway?"

"Juan," he said.

"Mucho gusto," I replied and left it at that.

Such goes the conversation these days,
they just plunge right in
without a hint of being phased.

Boys

All I keep hearin' 'bout is
how them boys have problems
with us so called "bitches."
But let me set a few things straight.
Yeah, I'm gonna smoke a few past you,
quicker than them major league pitches.

They say we hoes if we do it on the first night,
but if reversed,
dudes be praised for
stickin' it to her right.
Don't matter if she put up a fight.
He's considered a stud flyin' higher
than a kite while smokin' some bud.

Man, that shit whacked,
I mean if I wanna smack it to him
even from the back it don't mean I'm dirty,
just real sturdy and ready for a full-fledged attack.

Girls got needs too,
the difference is
we do it more tactfully.
Sometimes we act shy,
but we sly,
don't be fooled by our innocent eyes.
We know how to play the game too.
Maybe better
'cause we don't need a pat on the back
when it's all through.

What's up with the lines they throw,
thinkin' it will make jaws drop
and juices start to flow?
Here's a line I got in '94.

"Baby, you look so fine

I wanna take that elevator
and ride you up and down all night long."

I mean, c'mon!
Is that the most romantic shit ya got?
That doesn't make me want to hit it on the spot.

And you know them rumors be flyin' too,
especially the ones back in high school.
He said, "Sarah, yeah, she pleased me
even though she was so fuckin' easy."

But in the back of his mind
he knows the truth,
the man did not make it
home like Babe Ruth!

She teased his ass
then ripped some gas
and left him alone to breathe it.
But no one hears that side of things
'cause home boy has an ego to swing.

So we take it and ya know we fake it,
but it don't stop ya fools from shakin' it.

Once I thought a man was sincere,
telling me I was the prettiest girl he'd seen all year.
Until the next week
when I caught him in the club throwin' that line to Cristina,
like, a sorority girl from the Valley in Cali.

They say they ain't players but, man,
I'd rather be called a bitch than
be a dude with no control of his dick
and listen to the shit they be throwin'.

So that's it folks,
that's all I got,
Bitch #1 cleansed her soul
and is ready to rock.

Don't get me wrong,
I love them boys,
just not the ones with
them tricky ploys.

Passion

Passion, excess passion inside. It burns exorbitantly. It's longing to be released to the right person. Overwhelming, all-consuming and waiting.

> Dangerous, but then that's what makes passion so exhilarating. The danger, the excitement of releasing so much of ourselves. It obliterates all that is rational.

With passion is love too, which makes it doubly strong if the two are combined, but that much more meaningful,
sublime.

> I will just have to wait and let the passion continue to bundle and burn until I find that someone who is able to untangle and release the yearn.

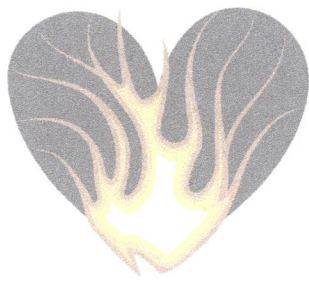

Image from Microsoft Word 2010

Duplicity of Love

The duplicity of lovingly
loving you
without hypocrisy.

The duplicity of lovingly
loving you
throughout eternity.

How can I love you when I don't like you?
Is liking you required to love?
Hypocrite they call me,
but I can't explain,
falling deeper and deeper to the point of pain.
As I mask my heart from the blow,
I continue to hear these words just flow....

The duplicity of lovingly
loving you without hypocrisy.
The duplicity of lovingly loving you unconditionally.

My thirst for love cannot be quenched. Luckily, your love for me is forever replenished.

The duplicity of lovingly loving you unconditionally.

The duplicity of you lovingly loving me throughout eternity.

Open The Door

It was morning and I opened the door to see the sun shining brightly through the clouds of gray. And even though you told me we could never be, the world still looks good to me.

I open my door to you, 'cause we've shared so much oh you know it's true. It would be a waste to not forgive and get through. The loss of a friend will never be what I look forward to...so I'm starting anew, and I open my door to you.

I am stronger than I knew I could be. Perhaps you gave me that, perhaps I just grew. Just listen to these words and give them a chance, I'm looking to keep a friend and build on the past.

The choice is yours, this I know, but no matter what decision you make please know, you have a friend forever in me and a place to call home.

Intangible

It's locked inside because you suffocated it in me.
It really wanted and still wants to breathe,
but it's shy,
uncertain,
afraid of being lured and deceived again.

Its eyes were closed before when it thought it could see "crystal" clear.

But the crystal was blemished and shattered, due to your hand, in a million, make it a trillion pieces. And now, it doesn't know how to form again, so it can have the ability to see perfectly.

Don't feel bad though, I really don't believe you did it intentionally. But maybe, for once, you should have used some forethought and looked at how the situation was in development. Without you in the center, the focus of every picture.

That's not the way you are though, it knows this at last, but kept looking past hoping there was more in you to share. It still doesn't know exactly what to think, it's unfair, confused, like an innocent child who doesn't understand why they feel the blues. Is that what you wanted, were you afraid of facing the truth?

Because of you it is a lost prisoner struggling, searching to be set free from this cage from which you enslave.

Maybe it was its fault after all.
Should have listened to the gut feeling that echoed every day,
echoed every day without end,
end, end, don't believe it's gonna end.

So naïve, and now doesn't know which direction to turn. It stays lost, locked, and suffocating in that cage. Will it ever be alive again, or just age and age?

Uncovered

He looked me in the eye
and gave me a choice,
albeit as a child without a voice.

He knew it was manipulative and dirty.
He asked if I wanted to switch places,
but I was too weak, too unsteady.

I declined,
and didn't do
what I should have done.

Sinister in his way,
he knew exactly what to say.
To make me feel low and responsible in a way.

I cried.
I cried out for anyone who was outside.
But he told me he'd give me something for which to cry.

So powerless I laid unsafe under my covers,
tears streaming down my face until they vanished,
never to be discovered.

Until the adult me suddenly,
so lovingly,
allowed them to be uncovered.

Blue Jeans and Black Shirt

She told me blue and black don't go together.
Blue and black, black and blue,
maybe I wear the colors on the outside
as a symbol of my hurt on the inside.

> Blue and black, black, and blue,
> the colors represent pain beneath the skin,
> and reveal the hurt peering through.
> Black and blue marks for the whole world to see,
> the colors seem to go so well together naturally.

Pain from stupidity, maybe a drunken night
where I bumped into a table or got in a fight.
Pain from anger, punching a wall
or taking an unexpected fall.
Maybe from sadness and misunderstanding,
cutting and bruising myself to make sense of it all
and forever demanding...... attention.

> This is its voice, its way to be seen.
> Pain from depression
> using aggression to cope with it all,
> the blue and black,
> black and blue,
> remind me that I am still alive,
> standing, functioning, not invisible,
> and I'll see this through.

These colors are below my epidermis.
If I choose to wear them on the outside of my skin
purposefully dispatched and patched,
don't tell me they don't fucking match.

A Single String

I wander through crowds and

observe humanity

yet choose to stay on the outskirts

for some unexplained insanity.

Like when you strum

a single string

on a guitar.

I am loud and confident and

sound perfectly in pitch

but not knowing

by being inclusive of the other strings

there's true beauty and depth

and such richness.

Screen Doors

"Always peering through a screen door."
That's what she said to herself.

You see that's the way she always felt.
As the outsider who's peering in.

But not completely outside,
like with a regular door
made of wood
where someone is completely shut out,
unable to peer in.

It was a screen door.

She could still feel a part of it all,
still smell the atmosphere,
and still see through that screen,

so, in essence
they could still say she was there,
and she could too.

But she wasn't.

Shut out by that slight grayness
and thin wire that separated
them from her.

Perhaps she put it there herself.
Imaginary shields to protect
herself in some way.

Or was it they
who didn't really want her in on their small soiree?

She didn't really know;
all she knew is that

even if a room was roaring with noise and laughter
and filled with people
she still felt lonely and
an afterthought.

Not alone though,
just like an outsider looking in.

In some ways it was better.

She could observe and get a feel
for who people really were.
Maybe that's why those screens were there....
Until she felt she knew them,
trusted them,
and felt they deserved to see more of her,
only then would she remove the screen.

But if it is they who put it there,
she guesses she will have to live
never really being a part of a specific circle.
Forever on the periphery
bouncing from one to the other
entering then exiting.

"It's not necessarily a bad thing,"
she thought to herself.

She just hopes she doesn't get used to it
because then she will grow to a point of
never really needing anyone.

She will condition herself
to never really knowing
or letting anyone else truly
know her.

Telephone Lines

Electric impulses connected him to me.
Electric impulses,
at first touch,
sent raging through me.

With so much distance,
wires connected us.

The sound of his voice eased my soul and filled my
heart with intense glee.

The telephone lines worked so perfectly
back then.

Never really having to deal with
the everyday issues that rack up
and really test the relationship.

After just a phone call
I thought I knew him
because of how he made my heart swell
with joy and connection.

How wrong I was,
so fooled and tricked.
I thought words could close the gap
of miles and make us tick.

I thought I could know him,
trust who I thought he was,
but the reality is we add much to the narrative,
we fill in the unknown,
making the person who we want them to be.
He did it with me too,
even if he didn't admit it.
I knew it from the start,
I should have listened to my gut.

The telephone lines
connected us,
and perhaps that was all that did?

My heart says no, that can't be true
because it would skip a beat at the sound
of the ring on the hook.
But my mind says,
Yes,
it likely is,
when I examine the delicate,
thin,
and unreliable lines
of
the
telephone.

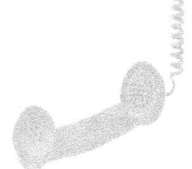

Touch

The remnants of his touch
still pulsated through my body.

The second he left
I yearned for him more.
Even though he wasn't here anymore,
I still felt him caressing my entire body,
erasing every worry,
easing every muscle.

Whispers of sweet nothings
still echoed in my ears.

I was in withdrawal
after only one night with him,
not sex,
just his soul and mine connecting.
Withdrawal almost until
the point of tears.

"Let myself have these feelings,"
I say to myself, "Go with it."
"If all fails, it fails,
but for now,
enjoy your place and time with him."

Soñando Contigo

(Spanish version, the English translation is on the next page.)

Soñando contigo.
Tu sonrisa, tu andar,
tú manera de ser y tu adorable aroma intoxicante.
Mi corazón no para de volar.

Tú me dijiste
que yo tenía tu corazón en mis manos.
¿Como?
Yo no sé,
tus palabras no llevan razón.

Contigo a mi lado
siento tranquilidad y paz completa.
Espero que tus episodios impulsivos
solo sean pasos del tiempo y no van a ser repetidos.
Mis preocupaciones cesan de existir,
tú me haces completa.
El hueco que sentía yo tú me lo has llenado tan fácil,
tan sencillamente.

Tú dices que eres mi juguete por el momento.
Que voy a jugar contigo por un rato y después botarte en el suelo.

Ay mi amor,
mi negrito como puedo explicarte
que los juguetes no me fascinan.
Tú me fascinas más que las estrellas que brillan.
Tú has capturado
mi corazón y me has enseñado como abrirlo a tu amor.

Yo creo en ti y siempre voy a sentirme así.
Nunca olvides el valor y el poder que tienes
cuando entregas tu amor.

Dreaming of You

Dreaming of you,
your smile, your gait,
your way of being and your lovely intoxicating scent.
My heart won't stop from flying.

You told me
I had your heart in my hands.
How?
Your words do not bring with them reason.

With you at my side
I feel tranquility and complete peace.
I hope your impulsive episodes
are only fleeting passages of time
and that they are not repeated.
My worries cease to exist.
You make me feel whole.
The hole I once felt
you have filled so simply and easily.

You say that you are
my toy for the moment.
That I am going to play with you
for a bit and then throw you in the dirt.
Oh my love,
my brown one,
how can I explain to you
that toys don't fascinate me.

You fascinate me more than the stars shine.
You have captured my heart and
you have shown me how to open it up to love.
I believe in you and I will always feel this way.
Never forget the worth and power
you have when you give your love.

Sin to Love You

They made me feel that it was a sin to love you.
Is it possible to love someone too much?
Love so grand it becomes too big and hard to control?
Like a rumor that takes on a life of its own.

When we started it was sweet like honey, so sticky,
and innocent as a lamb,
so pure.
We were perfectly imperfect.

But like rumors,
the drama started to brew.
Were we secretly trauma bonding
or just bonded to the trauma
without even knowing it?
Trauma drama.

I know we are in bondage to sin,
but love?
My experience of the four-letter word
was different from that definition as was yours.

I'm held in bondage to that other four-letter word
that begins with the letter F.
The loss of control,
so familiar for some reason.
A season of my past,
left within the subconscious....
unconscious,
dormant.

That can't be what drew us to each other!
It felt right and true,
now so surreal that the new definition is unreal.
I don't want to believe it.
I think I've just created it to create more drama.

Love is blind.
I knew love could hurt,
but hurt like that?

It shows up in mysterious ways.
It knows no bounds.
Perhaps that is why the lines of
love and pain and comfort
are blurred.

No boundaries are to be had,
and that doesn't sound so absurd as
love conquers all.

Love is patient,
love is kind.
Love has no end.
Endless love.

But love hasn't always been kind to me or you.
It leaves our definition rightly skewed.
It's mixed up in a ball of aching delight.
Rolling on, around and literally through.

It leaves me with a hole that's impossible to fill
and my heart oozes love like lava
flowing from a volcano.

Sometimes so heavy and crushing,
sometimes so tender and healing,
and sometimes so painful
it's like a lightning bolt
sent through my entire being.

I'm simultaneously electrified and electrocuted.
The chispa, the spark,
we always had has left my heart
burnt to a crisp from feeling its utter bliss.

In order to save myself
do we need to part?

Or in order to save you
is it death do us part?

We started something we just can't stop.
Sinners or winners,
we have to choose.
Choose between each other or
our very selves we could lose.

It doesn't have to be that way....
the choice is ours,
it's the price we'll have to pay.
If it's a sin to love you,
then let us bow our heads and pray.

Anguish

Some days I feel so hard
it hurts.

That kind of aching that
builds a lump in your throat and
pressure in your chest and
behind your eyes.

An empty kind of hurt
because you aren't sure exactly
why or where
the feeling
is stemming from.

Persistent insidious hurt.

My eyes resist
to see the root,
but I still feel it so hard
it hurts.

Self

I treasure the moments of solace and quiet.
And wonder if tomorrow will bring
new respite from the feelings that are
so dark and heavy and full of self-doubt.

The quiet moments also bring me hope
that things will be different.
I will reframe and reclaim and
be ahead of the game
for once. The shame
won't fill me to the brim.

Grim,
forbidding,
uninviting.

Uninviting, I like that word.
These feelings are *uninvited*,
not allowed,
but they still remain....
so profound.

I'm forbidden from speaking
because if I did,
it would be too selfish.
So I flush it......however,
it doesn't die.

The self will endure
somewhere
until the end of time.

Nothing is Something

Nothing, empty, void, hollow….
Not of hope,
or optimism though,
of something….. else.

Just a feeling.
Something is stealing….
Something is robbing me
of a piece of life that longs for peace.

Perhaps I'm addicted to the internal drama.
Perhaps I can't let something go.
Something is there.
Always there, peering deep into my soul.

Telling me to just let go,
let it go, let it go,
just be one
with the wind and sky….
As you so very well know
how the familiar song lyric goes.

But is that something there for you?
Or does it leave you alone?
Something tells me,
this one's unique to me.
Made for me, likely by me,
in the fragments of my mind.
Not patched together like a nice,
organized quilt made
complete over time.
But even patches alone can be beautiful,
no?

I don't want to wilt at the guilt
of this something ever present.

Be it banished
to the edges, the fringe,
since it doesn't just vanish.

The pain felt by this something leaves a mark.
But the mark I make soothes me with a pain
of which I can predict.

I control,
I know when it comes and
feel comfort from the familiar blows.

Perhaps this is something I have merited.
Perhaps my something will
eventually diminish into nothing one day?
Perhaps it's here to stay?

My hope is its taunt will decrease
and its haunt will cease.
That it will stop making my body its home
and mind a cell
where I'm trapped in some sort of hell
where the boogeyman and demons dwell
and wait.

Will I continue to fall for the bait?

Wait……..

but it's nothing……..

That's still something.

Made of Glass

Shut up,
don't tell him
that he doesn't deserve to see
a cherished side of me
or hear my inner voice.

I have a choice,
purge my insides to everyone with an ear,
or be selective with my audience
to only a few with a close up view?
I have nothing to hide,
so why keep it in?
Oh wait,
yes I do.

The more who hear
the more feedback I get.
Maybe I set myself up for heartache,
but better me than them.
In the end,
I will be twice as strong.

I'm made of glass;
everyone can see right through me.
I have so many secrets,
take a glance.
I am open for all to see.
Perhaps you think this fills me
with vulnerability?

It probably does.

Hard on the outside, empty within
this is who I am.
I can see through me too.
I know it will only take one rock
to shatter that protective outside wall,

and when the pieces fall to the ground,
I will pick myself up
and face the truth.

Sticks and stones will break my bones
and on the way down
the names will hurt too.
Whomever said they could never hurt was strongly mistaken.
I will feel forsaken.

Like I said before, when my glass is shattered,
I'll pick myself up and build myself anew
of something stronger this time,
maybe hardwood.
And when they chop through me,
I will build myself of steel,
and when they burn and melt me down,
I will find something different
with which to rebuild.

It will never end,
and I will continue to fight and conquer.
So, I choose to be made of glass
at this point,
but intentionally, as it will force me
to be better and maybe
the fall hurts less every time.

Like calluses that form in place of a wound.
Even the ones unseen.

Soft Heart

They tell me I have a soft heart.

Perhaps......

.... soft in my ability to give compassion to those that do the most harm.

.... soft in my ability to cry with such intensity at the little things in life that charm.

.... soft in my ability to insert myself into someone else's position, to understand what they are going through with every tough transition.

.... soft in my desire to serve others and the world without conditions.

.... soft in my ability to turn the other cheek even though I feel so incredibly wronged, by someone who put a knife through my soft heart *killing me softly* like the song.

I'd rather have a soft heart than one that's been hardened by the grind.

For what good are hard hearts that serve for little growth and that bind?

A hard heart may protect me from getting hurt, that is true.

But then that isn't really living life then, is it?

Which one will you choose?

Part II: The Battle

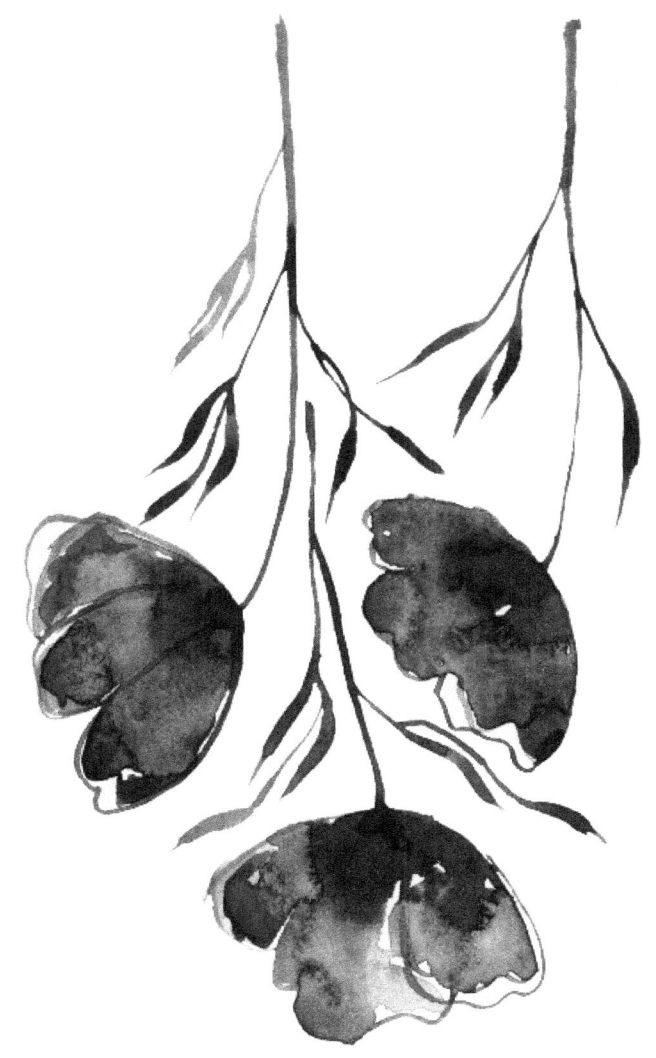

Pieces

She lost who she was,
so she set out for herself to find.
Winding through the halls of her past,
finding pieces scattered,
left behind.

Maybe, she thought,
if she found enough pieces,
she could glue them together
and feel whole again like a masterpiece.
At least look whole.

Wait,
that isn't the problem,
she looks complete,
oh yeah,
she puts on the show.
She does this so
nobody will know,
so no one will feel
the pain she feels
or see how sad she really is.

She does this so the looks
don't crash down on her.
You know the ones,
with their eyes that judge,
they are around every corner
waiting to punch.

She's like the *Truman Show*
without the true.
Her story has holes in it,
they see this too.
Her show is so she is liked
and not cast aside
like a cigarette butt

thrown out the window to fly at night.

It protects her
from those who hurt her from outside,
and perhaps, the ones inside too.
Safe where they aren't seen.
The façade protects them
but tears her apart.

Searching for her pieces,
like a puzzle to be made complete.
When finally, as one
it will be so satisfying,
so redeeming, such a relief.

She wonders,
will she need to let the wild ones out
and face them to feel at peace?

She doesn't want to vanish and be invisible.
She will break through;
she will break free
and heal the broken pieces of me.

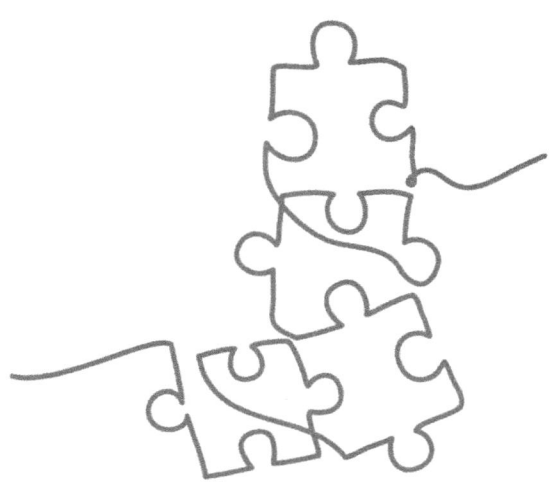

Mirror Mirror

You tell me to think,
to have confidence,
but how can I do so
with your constant condescendence?
The chubby little tubby
with too many moles,
with socks full of holes
and silly little freckles.

You think you own me?
I rise above you.
Yet you hover and lurk,
I see your smirk.
Smirky jerky quirky little girl.
You try to stare me down until I say no contest.
Well, I protest.
I protest, I say!

You compare me to that which you think
is weak, ugly, and shameful inside.
I twist your reality and say this weakness you see;
this weakness is gaining strength by the second,
this ugly is another's beauty,
and this shame is nothing more than self-doubt.

Oh yes, we play this game often
and I know I'm not the only one.
I wink at you, and you wink back.

You maybe had me convinced for a second,
but a second won't last as long as it takes me
to blow you the quick kiss of death.

Quirky clever little smarty pants
just outwitted the cheap pathetic silenced voice inside.
Until we meet again my foe.

Nightmare

Disguised,
you knocked
on the doors of my brain tonight.
I let you in
and now the real fun begins.

No sleep,
tossing and turning.

The constant yearning
for silence and not that record
that plays on repeat.

Sometimes someone else knocks
and I open the door ever so slowly,
trembling with fear wondering
who/what is on the other side.
"Who's there?" I ask.

Sometimes my friend,
distraction, comes for a visit,
but that's usually short lived
as they don't stay very long
for obvious reasons......Oh!
There's that record again,
I hear it in the background
with its familiar and menacing sound.

Ding dong,
a doorbell this time!
Who/what could be on the other side?

As I slowly open the door
I hear the eerie creak,
shuddering and shaking
as I peer around to take a peek.
This time it is guilt paying me a visit,

for no reason at all and without invitation.
I feed guilt some dinner
and hope they will go away,
but they stay listening
to that record play.

Restless, uneasy,
and full of guilt,
anxiety arrives
and joins the social mix.

This shameful combination
of guests is an
intoxicating concoction of insomnia at its finest.
No rest is allowed
with this crowd.

Just when I'm about to doze off,
I hear the familiar knock.

While I lethargically open the door,
I shudder and shiver at the monster I see,
as the monster peering back is a clone of me.
She's grasping that same record
with the maniacal smile of Joker's glee.

Convicted and condemned
because of her own convictions,
she's ready to play with the darkness again.

Bound to repeat this record
as she drifts *off*
to never never land.

Museum of My Identity

I thought I knew who I was.

So full of life and aspiration.
>So positive and hopeful,
>gratified,
>meeting expectations.

Then you came along and now I'm left
wondering, searching because who I once was, is no more.

Left confused and befuddled are you attempting
>to settle some kind of score?
>Like a scorned partner who has been betrayed,
>you've gutted me,
>I'm slain.

I spend days looking at versions of me in the mirror.
>It's as if I'm walking through the mirror to find myself on the other side, wandering around a museum of my identities and I'm unable to hide.

I pull one off the rack and try it on for size.
>Sometimes it fits
>much to my surprise!

Maybe like this the variety keeps me going and matches my mood.
>Maybe like this I feel whole and less subdued?

It kind of feels like a circus though and some sort
of punishment.
>I'm my own muse for my own
>aMUSEment.

Do you think you can open the door and let me out?
>I see my real ID just right over there, within arm's reach,
>pristine in condition,
>not to be compared.

But all you'll let me do is
        stare.

My hands can't touch nor place it on,
so I continue to wander
and just
press on.

Intertwined

Upon first sight, it felt like the beginning.
Beginning of hope, the beginning of……
us.

The beginning of something so special.

Your beautiful smile and cute demeanor had me drawn
to you with some sort of unexplainable magnetism.

But then I saw the other side of you,
so quick to anger,
so mean, so possessive, and
disrespectful.

I thought it despicable
how you treated your mom.

But deep inside I felt your
heart was something different.
Noble, caring, loving,
below the hard exterior.

You picked the worst
they told me.
I didn't believe what they said
and I still don't.

But then you lied
and lied again.
You didn't try
and you humiliated me.

But then you apologized and assuaged me.
A true *Dr. Jekyll and Mr. Hyde*.
But that did not stop us
from continuing on our rocky path.
You hurt me and hurt me some more,

your hands on my neck,
leaving me with invisible sores.

"I won't do it again," you promised me then,
your words are just as harsh,
they always have been.

But you make me feel as though
you'd take a bullet for me, and you would.

You gave me your heart,
your love for me is never ending.
This was evident from the very start.

I looked past it and moved on with love.
Then you did it again and again and I put up with it.
Is this pattern intertwined from our pasts?
Inevitably we keep repeating it blast after blast?

Not sure what to do as our love is true
and these behaviors don't reflect the real you.

I lost who I was somewhere along the way
and melted into you, complacent,
focusing on babies to raise.

I put up with the abuse,
because of your valid excuse,
deciding to move forward
believing in love each day.
Intertwined we stay.

Temptation

I met the devil today.
Oh, he had me a dancin'.
Just threw me the chance
of power and complete control,
how could I say no?
I….had…..it…..all,
and was havin' a ball.

I had all the money in the world
including yours.

Anything I ever wanted to be or see I could,
anyone I wanted to take revenge upon
I would.

It was so simple, it tickled my spirit
in a different way.

I was manipulative and secret,
how could I have allowed myself
to disintegrate to something so low as this?

The devil tempt *me* astray? No way!
Never! He put the gourmet tray
of life right in front of my face and I was weak
when put to the test.

That's not who I thought was my best.
My best is the least at last,
there was no getting past the man in red.

I sold my soul and will die worse in the end.
My final days will be alone with no one to trust.
How could I let myself crumble to dust?
Was I not taught better on how to resist
his lust and bust the devil away using his own dirty tricks?

Will I get another chance to climb out of fiery hell
or will the heat and pain at the top of life continue to swell?

Having it all has left me unfulfilled and bare.
No one cares and I don't blame them.
I wouldn't dare come close to me,
my sin and sickness may rub off
and I don't want the ill forced upon my will
pressed on anyone else I may cross.

Oh, the temptations of life have blinded me,
led me astray, away from truth so easily.

Perhaps a reminder of how fragile and distraught life can be?

I only hope now that it's true
that because one man gave his life,
the ultimate sacrifice,
human compassion revived,
that one day I am able to say
I survived.

Roots

There's a seed inside of you that grew and grew.
What you feel deep down in your gut are the roots.
> The roots of your unique you as they continually branch off,
> forming anew. The sweet sap of life pumping through
> every inch of your essence.

This must be nonsense; I'm writing of my own presence.
> How self-centered am I?

And yet, the more the roots grow and spread apart, the closer I am to knowing and better yet, being comfortable with me.

> Roots are the base, the epitome of a tree or plant's life;
> therefore, the deeper they are, the deeper the meaning.
> Yet harder to uproot and die when left in strife.

They do not move, break, or die.
> They just soak and seep in life. So wise they must be.

> Why then do I try to rip parts of them off? Am I trying to set a
> part of me free?

The deeper the roots the more secrets they yield. Secrets meant to be covered and concealed.
> I don't want to peel at them to know who I am, better to rip
> them out from their bitter cemented dirty place that I hope will
> never be revealed.

These stray roots may not contain the pride I once thought, but the older ones are the true me that are so thick they won't let me forget. It's time to be reminded and remember the good person full of gentility.

> It's time to plant good seeds so I can blossom full of love,
> understanding and tranquility.

'Round and 'Round

Complete and utter exhaustion.
I love the feeling of knowing I have
worked every fiber in my body to the core.
Rip, stretch, pull, push.
Pain shooting, I do not think I can do more.

But I continue, "mind over body" I say to myself.
My mind and body are having a fight,
but "the mind always wins"
a sergeant once told me.

Full exhaustion means a full night's sleep.
Not able to have energy to worry or think
or be concerned about the little things.

Just sinking into the sheets; they swallow me whole and spit me out the next morning renewed and vital for a day to expend energy once again.

Ever looked at life that way?
Live to expend and attain energy,
that's our purpose?
Does that mean I've failed if I'm fidgety and restless, unsatisfied when the day is done?
Maybe the wheel will never finish being spun.

We go 'round and

                    'round and

                        'round

                        without end

                      or true completion

                                  to be found.

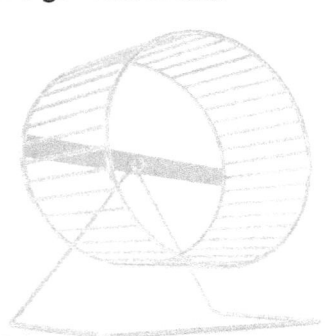

Shadow

The shadow lurks.
It gently and persistently pulls.
The devil whispers in my ear.

Tune it out with distraction and activity; yet it's always there.

In the quiet moments of solace,
it quickly pounces to rob me of any moment of real peace.

Inner voices of self-hatred and paralyzing anguish.

"You're not worthy."

"That's what
you deserved."

Painful thoughts
and images surround.

The shadow is working hard
to conquer my spirit.

Don't let the pain bleed out onto others,
work hard to cover your stained path.

Show no weakness.
Show no meekness.

The pain within shall not infect those surrounding you.
Do what needs to be done.

Adapt and overcome.

Soldier on.

Lost

To capture a feeling without words,
and if I could draw as an artist does,
I'd draw a picture of a person in my chest.

You'd see a second image of them,
their face, anguished and screaming out
in pain and discomfort from the uneasiness coming
from inside but somehow silenced.

This uneasiness of being in their own skin.

On their face though you will see a smiling person
trying to be brave and happy for those loved ones around them.

Trying to be a good parent, trying to keep it together
to make a living for their family. It's getting harder
and harder to be that person these days.

Sometimes they feel they've gone so deep inside themselves they
don't know who they are anymore.

They've lost themselves and then they wonder if they ever knew
themselves to begin with.

Who they once were, is no more.

Out of the Gray

A cloudy state of mind
amidst worries in the world.

Anxiety from political and social unrest,
injustice, general division and
polarity, mounting stress from trying
to make ends meet while this virus we navigate
and try to defeat.

Fires, floods, hurricanes,
global warming all swarming
and sadly, norming.

Amid this mind fog,
I hear some yelling and screaming and
laughter coming from the distance outside
that pulls me out of the gray.

I get up to see what's going on.
The joy of the first snow, the joy of first play,
the joy of community and parents and children
together at the end of a day.

The first snowfall brings back those fond feelings
and I remember the fun.
Perhaps it's a survival mechanism of sorts,
an innate and instinctive elevation of my senses,
but I'll take it
because slowly, surely, we'll see through
these challenging times by paying attention to
these sorts of simple and pure joys.

Wicked Sea

Diving into the depths of a wicked sea,
swimming through
an abyss of nothingness.
Nerves on edge,
muscles tight,
blood spiked high
with confusion on the horizon.

Should I ride the current or fight upstream?
If I fight, will I have the strength?
Will I have the stamina to continue to push?

It feels like a weight is shackled to my leg,
pulling me down sharply leaving its mark
with an indented ring around my ankle.

Insidious.

While on the surface I flutter,
pretending to hold my head above water.
Will someone come to my rescue?
Will someone pull me up?
Or will the current pull me asunder?

Dare I scream PLEASE at the top of my lungs?
I peer down at my reflection and what do I see?
I scream back, "Don't look at the surface so
superficially!"
I look again, this time deep into the green
eyes of my soul,
time moves in slow motion,
and there deep within,
can you see?

Image from Microsoft Word 2010

I whisper softly to the sweet breeze.
There burns the fire. With a kind of
warmth, I yearn to give, a warmth full of
vulnerability.

This vulnerability is the catalyst to such a tumultuous ride.
WE must ride, for you are me and I am you, the faces of
humanity, not knowing what pain or what joy may come next.

Come what may, we must ride during highs, and we must ride
through lows and on and on it goes.

Dirty Dishes

At your body's core,
your sense of self has been so buried
by feelings of worthlessness
it's hard to dig through.

You dig to the top,
oh wait,
not the top,
just another layer.

Dirty layers don't seem to end.
It's like when you wash dishes in a dishwasher.
Sometimes when you go to put them away,
you hesitate
because you don't remember if they're
clean or dirty anymore;
it's been so long that you've kept them inside.

You just assume they're dirty.

When will I be able to put my dishes away?

In Between

        I feel I'm stuck in between.

In between worlds.
        Not completely urban and
        not country enough either.

Not conservative and definitely not
liberal enough, at least to them.

        Not dumb, just not smart enough.

A strong leader but not enough to get me where I want to go.

        Where was that exactly?

Confident but just not quite enough.

        Athletic but not consistent enough.
        A chameleon with no real home.

Like a Xennial somewhere between a Gen X and a Millennial.

        Religious but not enough for the church.
        Friendly but not friendly-faced enough.

Accepting but not self-accepting enough.

        Enough is enough.

At least in between is somewhere.

        Right?

Uneasy

It's that uneasy.
The uneasiness you feel at the pit of your stomach
like when hunger strikes or blood sugar plummets.

Uneasiness of your nerves just as when cartoonish
squirmy squishy worms suddenly zapped by a taser
become straight as a toothpick or razor.
Uneasy feels easier when busy.

Perhaps it's the constant churn and burn
as the world turns.
A turn at your same frequency
that makes it more comforting.

Like a Johnny Cash beat,
you hear the train a comin',
at that hypnotizing pace... at any rate you wait......
for peace.

Peace of mind, of heart, of soul.
Pieces of you restored to a whole.
You speak in fragments just as certain
memories are remnants of something
that was taken forsaken and devoured.
Innocence taken like a wilted flower,
or the impending apocalypse of tomorrow,
it lies there with your sorrow.

Now you've dwelled in the deep dark well too long,
time to climb up, brush it off and move along.
Come with me, button it up and stand erect,
so no one will suspect the uneasy lives inside making you feel like the
chief suspect.

Yet I suspect, they expect it's a phase,
a haze, a daze of days gone by.
The uneasiness comes at a price

but isn't it nice
to be worth something and not have to think twice
and roll the dice on life?

At what price, at what cost?
All
is
NOT
lost.

Just uneasy.

Saving Smile

Her sweet smile never let her down.
As long as she put that smile on every day, she knew
she'd get through.

It functioned as her armor.
The armor that forced her to be brave.
Nobody saw below the surface of that smile,
below the surface where the storm that brewed
all day everyday gained momentum and was waiting
to be unleashed.

Or perhaps she was afraid they did and could
see right through her.

They could see that ugly storm, her ugly storm.
Either way, the smile would somehow
get her through, she thought, as usual.

Until it didn't,
and she felt betrayed and let down.

Lost in her thoughts, she hardly remembered who she was.

Then forced herself to learn to laugh at life and
she found her smile, her armor again
and was able to press on.

The Boogeyman

I will swallow you whole, you just wait, you will succumb.
YOU HAVE NO POWER OVER ME. YOU are the problem.

The problem is you actually *think* you do. *"Don't let me get me, I'm a hazard to myself."* Those are the words of your life.

You are truly the *black swan* getting ready to be set free, the day will come, just wait and see.

Controlled chaos.
Remember the picture you would draw? Remember the numbness? Remember me? You ARE me.

Pretend I'm not here, pretend I'm not real, pretend you can overcome my choke hold.
Pretend I'm gone even.
You imposter.

Imposter in every aspect of the word. I'm the real you.
You are but a slimy fish floundering under the tip of my thumb. Flip flop, flip flop until you drop into the cold depths of darkness.
Blackout.

Just mortal flesh, feel my presence, my heavy presence, penetrating you with my venom, sucking you dry, until you have no more tears left to cry, as you are mine.

Transformed, transfixed, and asphyxiating.
Inhabiting your mind
and body
and soul
and will never
EVER
let you go.

Yin and Yang

Just write, a letter, a word.
A thought.
Let it explode on paper.
But it doesn't.
I'm carrying a ton of bricks
ready to crash one minute
and then upon the click of a trigger
at the start of a race, I'm
running a marathon.
Energizer bunny one minute,
paralyzed the next.
Pull and push,
yin, and yang,
good and bad,
heavenly and evil.
Which one am I?
Am I who I thought I always was or
will a part of what makes me special
go away once it's
healed?

Drip Drip

Drip, drip, drip
just like the tick tick tick
of time.

Don't let it slip, slip, slip by,
don't let it consume.

Sip, sip, sip
numbing all the ugliness inside.

Am I where I should be?
Doing all of the things I need to be?
Or should I let it be?
Is this the right path?

Drip, drip, drip,
tick, tick, tick like a bomb,
waiting to explode.
Will I implode or explode?
Will I be all I can be?
Who am I anyway?

Tick, tick, tick
help me find me,
lick, lick, lick of his fingertip, tip, tips.
Marking me as his for life,
shattering my reality.

        Tick...... tick........ tick..........

        time.............

        Heals.....
        Or does it?

        Tick.... tick.....tick.....

Red Lines

Imperfect red jagged lines, parallel train tracks
run up my right forearm and down my left.

The imprint is a reminder of weakness at its finest. The imprint, albeit temporary on the flesh, is ever present in the abstract corners of my mind.

Envision a train trying to run down those tracks,
such a bumpy and uncomfortable ride.

But the train keeps moving through at its deliberate pace. I hear the consistent chug and squeal of its sturdy iron wheels. It doesn't falter at the bumps and jerks of the track ahead and continues to plow through.

An analogy of that which I must continue to do. Chug along, imperfect tracks imparted or not, I must continue the work and not stop.

If the train is me and the pain and hurt are the tracks, we must coexist to keep moving forward and STAY on track.

I am like the train, relentless in my determination and resolve to heal.

Labyrinth of Life

My arms stretch forward before me as I walk through a forest of trees.

Their branches pull me here and there through a chaotic maze.
A labyrinth full of obstacles to defeat.

The maze goes on and on like my mind twisting and turning leading to nowhere in particular.

A journey to where?

Its twists and turns are making me dizzy.

Leading me blind with my eyes wide open.
I like the dark,
I like shadow,
to settle in unknown places that test my stamina.

How far into the deep dark can I go?
No one knows.

I hope this journey leads to a heart of love
and not to the heart of darkness that
currently consumes me.

I think I need a break,
to stop and sit in the slimy gloomy stench
 of it.

But I push forward carrying my weighted
feet forward until I collapse once more.

I'm getting weary.
So weary.
I slowly raise my head
and feel the warmth of the beautiful sun's rays on my face.
Life is so stunningly beautiful.

I bask in that spot and that thought and stay in that space.

My gaze falls upon the bright blue sky with puffy cotton candy clouds floating on by.

The gentle breeze calms my soul and I drift asleep forgetting where I was.

Then awake to what feels like a sharp slap across the face to the reality of this maze called life.

Warrior

A warrior.

A fighter.

It's who I am and I battle the war within daily.

I put on my war paint, hoping to suffocate any semblance of sadness or fear. It's a ritual of transition, a process.

I put on my paint and with each stroke I make
I am reminded that I can get through this
and not leave it to fate.

I long for the day when I feel as though I won't need the war paint.

Comfortable in my own skin, no insecurity within.

Society is as much to blame as I.
We teach girls to be good little girls in every way. Dedicated mothers and wives, in shape, smart, attractive, and successful.

But I'm a modern-day warrior. A warrior of the heart.
Always encouraging and pushing others to be their best selves.

I wish I could practice what I preach.
I reach and reach, grasping for the goal.
Until it's realized and a new one takes hold.

I pace with impatience in anticipation for the next.

A warrior.

A fighter.

Until I'm a conqueror.

Sink

In the quiet sometimes I let myself sink.
At first, I'm floating on the surface trying
to connect to the emotion deep within only
to find that demons await to remind me of
every sin.

They silently sleep most of the time but
move in and out of me on the sly.
Like.... cunning beings left unseen,
unnoticed.

Unless I pay close attention and connect
with the other side.
The warrior does get tired,
does give in.

I try to float above but sometimes let the heaviness set in.
I allow it to pull me under the slimy
surface until it envelops me.

I feel it in front and back and all around,
pulling me further and further down.
Heavier and heavier.
Sometimes I let it swallow me whole.
That old recognizable sensation, ironically
comforting in the familiar smothering
effect.

It's like I think I deserve the punishment, at least to some extent.
Will I be able to breathe there in the depths of its plunder?
Plunging so far into my soul eating me whole out from under?
I wonder if my war paint can save me today.
I wonder if my distraction can snap me out.
I scream and shout but I'm in too great of depths nobody can hear me.

Cleaning up my messy stained path wherever I go is getting weary.
Because I must be dirty, I must be an inconvenience.

I don't want to be a burden no matter where I go.

If I talk, I am, if I don't, I am.
What a conundrum.
Emptiness,
nothingness,
one dimension.
Feel something,
allow yourself to feel
in all dimensions.

Reflection

Smother me, choke out my voice.
There is a feeling deep down that wants to be heard and seen but doesn't know how to show itself.

It doesn't have the words to explain what the problem is.
Shame, anger, weakness, pathetic, sadness, emptiness, loneliness.

But I have to be strong. I have to set it aside.
I can't burden my friends. I can't burden my family.
My partner doesn't understand.

More shame.
I know what to say.
I know what to do.
It's the incongruent inside that's all over running askew.
I wish my "right" words were what I felt.
I wish my "right" words could be hung like a perfectly fitted hat on top of my head.

Wishes are good, they still keep me going.
But at what point does that stop?
After so long without coming to fruition wishes become empty aspiration and leave me feeling hollow,
searching for inspiration for tomorrow's tomorrow.

Left Right Left

Chaos controlled.
Left right left.
Am I losing my mind and soul?
Left right left.
Losing my grip.
Left right left.
I pick up my pace, I tighten the screws and forget my blues.
Left right left.

Solace in nature, feeling so deep,
silenced by trash, engaging in coping mechanisms so I can float away
from the past.
Left right left.

It's the superficial I hate.
This country is full of the superficial, and I want real.
Real love, real trust, real relationships. Those that love me for me,
flaws and all.
Left right left.

I am a warrior but need support.
Left right left.
Hopefully not that of life support
Where did I go?
Emptiness, nothingness, dying inside.
Left right left.

I smile on the outside to try to hide the hurt, but it's getting worse.
Left right left.
Trust the process, you are strong.
Left right left.

There is nothing wrong with being weak, just wait until you hit your
peak.
Keep climbing. Left right left.
Left right left...
I'm tiring of this pursuit!

Left right left
keep moving in your boots.

Left

right

left.

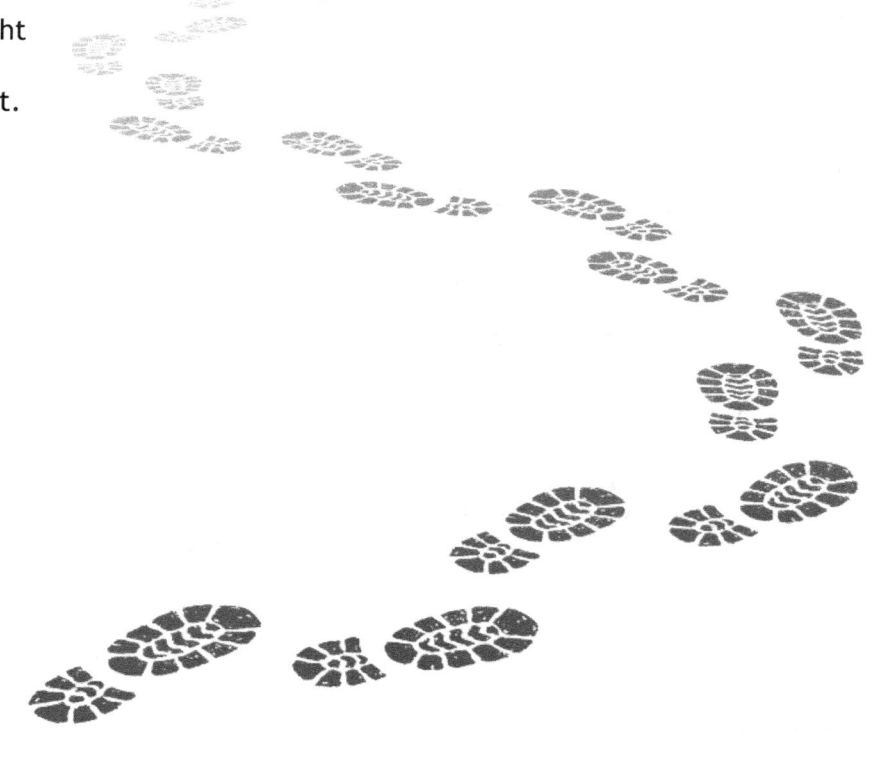

The Battle

The pull on my heart feels like an anchor's rope is strapped to the sides of the left and right ventricles while the anchor itself is being dragged through a weedy lake bottom.

Simultaneously, my daughter's laughter saves me instantly the moment I hear it. It lifts me up as if I were riding bubbles as they float and bob up through the sky.

Until the bubble suddenly pops,
and I fall hard.
Feelings so deep and profound,
so completely opposite.

Opponents sword fighting throughout the day and me the vessel through which their battle is carried out.

How do I drop in the middle of the battlefield and let all of that in?
How do I not fight in a battle that ensues daily?

The players change a bit as the vastness of feeling rushes in multitudes piercing through my soul.

If feelings were colors, a rainbow would wash through me.
The ability to feel is good,
as it means I'm not dead, I suppose.
It's the extremes that wear me out.
If I stop fighting the battle will my vessel be overcome?
Will I be trampled on? How will I live my life while meeting my expectations and those of others?

Accepting the abundance of human feeling and how it lives in me, I embrace with open arms.
Not really a choice ultimately as extreme feeling is part of me.
The choice to fight for life and living is mine though, and I do.
As I've said, I'm a warrior and have a warrior's heart.
Hoping I give myself grace the times I begin to sink from the pull of the weight.

I hope I find and reach out to the lifelines I need to arm myself against the opposing forces.

I best gather my tools as an artist does when carefully crafting a masterpiece. Whether on print with pen and ink, or digitally with my thumb, my words are one of my tools.

My masterpiece is to live proudly and true to me,
managing as the battle carries on,
in and around me.

The Demon Dance

We wrestle, you and I.
When I say you, I mean me.
I am the demon, and I am me.
I push you away and you push back. I remind you that I am a warrior and don't give in, I don't back down.

You remind me that you are slow to kill and will gradually suck the oxygen out, pulling me down until I have drowned.

"I'll swim harder", I remind the demon.

"And I'll let you swim", the demon replies back in a whim,
"Until you are so exhausted, you can't
push back. You can't win!"

"Then I'll sleep and regain my stamina,
I'm in this fight until the end," I exclaim!

"There is no end", the demon hisses back, "You're stuck with me for as long as you exist, I live as long as you do, I'm in the corners of your mind, and the deepest parts of your soul. I'm on the edge of your imagination robbing you of any control. I come out as I please, and with ease, I might add. I've been a part of you for as long as you've known."

"Okay, then maybe we ought to stop this dance. If this is what fuels you and puts me in a trance? Perhaps we can be friends and learn to live together side by side?" I ask.

Demon laughs, drool falling from her face. "Sure. Let's be friends. Let's give it a taste. We both know you fear me and from it I feed. My dear, a friend to you I am not, you should know better and just allow the onslaught."

"Never", I reply as I stare into her distant dark eyes. "This dance will continue, until I give my final battle cry."

And so, the dance proceeds. "Good thing I like to dance," is my final definitive remark, that I impart with a confident smile.

Demon sneers back.
I curtsy without hesitation.
We dance again.

Burn Away

I want the ugly parts of me to just burn away.
The parts that are soaked and seething
with decades of pent-up hurt.

Like when they would set bodies on fire in the water and push them
out to float.

The melodramatic, the emotional…. I suppose what I'd call
the messy human sides.

Just leave me with the perfect, unscathed, innocent parts.

As if those exist without the others?

Like the inside of a dark, cold, and abandoned rock cave, those parts
are dead inside. There is no life there.

So why not send them up in flames? They aren't serving me.

They are smothering me, and I want them gone.

I want to see their ashes smolder until they are lost and never found.

Why do they have to keep stringing me along?

Searching for the next dopamine fix, riding high on the waves of
adrenaline, nicotine, sugar, caffeine, really anything, even Netflix.

Fighting just to fight, with no real cause, always with you, who will put
up with the beast that doesn't belong.

But you are holding on way too tight.

You won't let those parts of me flow, float, and go.

Your fear is holding me back. So, it's myself I attack.

I'm backed in a corner, and I won't let anyone else have my back.

You should stop telling such tall tales. This isn't some sort of fairy tale.

You fucking tattle tale.

I think I might be asking too much.

Because I wonder if without those parts there'd be any human left?

Perhaps we can just try setting one piece out to sea to see how it burns and floats away from me?

So that I can live happily ever after.

And it may rest in peace.

Fire of Truth

The fire of truth starts to warm cold blood flowing through innocent veins.

When did my blood become cold?
When did we?

As the bottom of my heart is not,
is yours?

I would not have known the change
occurred had I not felt the warmth of the
fire's dangerous flame.

In life, change can come quickly
like a lonely wave rolling into the shore
and then suddenly it is no more.

You and I are here one minute
and then in a second
transform out of this place,
this time,
this space.

Good change can come slowly.
Like the flower that blooms in the spring
and the steady roll of a train on its tracks
leading reliably to the end of a trip.
The train still makes progress with
each steady spin of the wheel.

And while it may be the end of the trip...... it will not be
truly THE END.

Just one leg of the journey to the final destination.

The Yuck

The feeling is similar to when you are on a roller coaster, and you know the part where you are suspended in the air for a minute and your stomach goes up and is filled with anxious butterflies that swarm and tickle?

Then there's a split second of fear
upon descent and that feeling, although a second, feels like it lasts forever?

Then there's a sharp pull down, a crushing feeling from gravity.

The yuck feels like that but lasts much, much longer.
Imagine that feeling suspended for an unknown period of time.

Split

I'm methodical,
but also impulsive.

                    I'm happy go lucky,
                    but also depressive.

Calm on the exterior,
with a storm inside

                    Full of grace and
                    destruction all at the
                    same time.

Loved and loving.

                    Heartbreak. Shame.

Light.

                    Take flight.

Pendulum

Feelings and thoughts incongruent
Love and betrayal
running in
the
same
vein.
      Highs
           and
                 lows
                      swinging
                             like a
                                  pendulum,
                                       to and fro.
                                                  Controlled
                                           and chaotic
                                    wrapped up
                             in a
               storm's vortex;
         a reflection of
the goings on
          in the heart.
                    Pleasure
                        and pain
                              are synonyms.
                                         Happy
                                yet
                         full of
                             sadness.
              The impossible
       is possible,
possibly
         unexplainable
               Not probable.

                             But maybe...

Sharp Edges

Pieces of life found over time.
Not happy pieces,
painful pieces that want to gut me with their sharp edges.

Malevolent, dark, but shiny and sparkly to *pull me in*.
Reminders of good pieces of me are essential to *pull me through* the bedazzled pain, powerful.

Monumental moments that seem insignificant.

Significant time spent reminding me, remembering good.
Like fog rising from the lake in the morning, the sun burns the doubt away.

Momentarily.

I see the movement of love,
efforts of love.

I stay vigilant for the next sharp edge.

Yet it Shines

Total surrender or giving up?
Pushing, pushing, pushing, pushing; yet
never enough.

Fatigue from living out of my league.
A league where the best of the best live,
where they bring out the best in others and
always strive for more.

Like a firework blazing higher and higher in
the sky until it explodes from the pressure.
Beautiful in its descent, but it diminishes,
nonetheless.

Limited in how far it can rise.
What if it's defective/damaged?
Limited that much more,
not very far to soar,
yet it shines.

Haunting

Memories that bring back scary times.
Memories that haunt.
Memories that contradict that could also be true.

Like smoke that dissipates from a match, was it ever there?
Memories that I wonder were even real.
They haunt the corners of my mind
because I doubt they ever took place.

Memories of stolen innocence and disgrace.
Placing doubt in my mind, racing thoughts
over time.

Intertwined into a bundle of confusion and disbelief.
A thief of solitude and peace.

Never measuring up in a state of grief.

Relief. Relief from the haunt.

Distraught, as it's always there.

Irreverent. Daunting.

Haunting.

Little Wound

I have this little wound from long, long ago.

Pain

It didn't bother me much, until more recent times. When it broke through the invisible shield my subconscious fabricated to protect and keep me liberated.

Pain

The shield kept the source of the wound from eating its way to the surface. We kept it at bay, where we thought it would stay, and leave me impervious to the plethora of pain.

go

I'm not sure why this wound now festers and spits, but I think I created a stinky story
to go along with it.

away

A story that doesn't really fit, but then again, maybe it does?

come

No one knows for sure because it stays quiet and in the dark, only to peak its puny head out to awake suffering where it slumbered from the start.

again

The stench becomes overbearing though and I have nothing to gain by continuing to entertain the narrative the story has to impart,
but now that it's resurfaced,
it can't go back,
it will never from me part.

another

It's not a choice really; we live together in disharmony.

day.

I just need to stop agonizing over things that cannot be changed.

Pain

> For they are long past and it's best to leave them and treat them as murky dead remains.

pain

> The past is done and gone, and I must not stay stuck in the dissonance of the between.

go.

> As they are dreams that never were and unclear stories where the truth lies buried and blurred.

Just

> Buried in layers of the balance beam of who I'm supposed to or perhaps allow myself to be.

go

> If I just don't let myself go there everything will be fine. Go where though?
> There's nothing there to find.

away,

The bully is myself, why can't I just let myself out?

far

An unseen and unheard kind of doubt. The wound is but a manifestation of the unspoken macabre that's laid stake in this nowhere place. Embedded within a thick dark grey and green hazy forsaken mist.

away.

I'm injured and broken and there's no cure for this dream, no nightmare, that isn't allowed to exist.

Life

Trials and Tribulations
Joys and Jubilations
Sadness and frustrations
Smiles and transformations.
Life itself.

Chameleon

The company I keep dictates how I show up.

Coworker today, parent tomorrow, child/sibling the next, but do I know how to show up as my true self?

Fear of people knowing who I am, fear of them thinking I'm less than.

So, I adjust to the company,
only to let them so far in.

To protect who I am,
held deep inside,
deep within.

Protect

My love is so great I refuse to heal.

Protecting those closest from the blows I cannot reveal.

If the truth comes out, who will be left without?

Selfish ultimately.

Self-preservation.

Preservation of self.

It's a concept, self.

For I can convince you as to who I am as much as I can convince myself at any given moment.

One day one thing, another the next.

It's what I choose ultimately.
I choose the path of most resistance.

Perhaps it's comforting in a way.

I am both selfish and generous with this chosen *adventure*.

No good answer.

So, I take the one where the least will get hurt.

Even if that means me living with more.

Trapped

In a maze, in a haze embedded in my head. As I lay flat on my bed, words swimming around in space, losing track of time, losing track of me, losing the race as my head sinks further into the soft welcoming fabric of my pillow.

Afraid to say, afraid to stay.
Afraid not to say, afraid to leave.

I'm a thief of my own recovery and destiny.

A thief of peace and tranquility.
My own worst enemy. Cursed by my own hand, cursed because I say I am.

Don't let them in, but let them in. Distance yourself from what they show, the compelling story they tell, and the surge of urges you feel.

They are not real, just a figment strolling on by.
But to where exactly when they never seem to want to find a way outside. Cozy and comfortable staking claim in my mind. Lurking, waiting for the right time.

I can't let something not in that's already in.
I can't let it out without knowing how.
I'm boxed in repeating, repeating, repeating, repeating the same cycle.

Repeating, repeating, repeating, the same cycle.
Repeating, repeating, repeating, the same cycle.
Repeating.
Repeating.

Repeating, never enough.
Entrenched in a maze without a door.

Compartmentalized, sealed in an invisible box evermore.

With no escape in sight,
my unsettled weeping child keeps
repeating, repeating, repeating repeating…….

But, at least she can still see a thin stream of light.

Finding Myself

Bits of me are slowly being pulled away.
How and where I cannot explain.

It's scary.
It's kind of like a sparkler that slowly burns but then suddenly stops,
but much slower.
I'm losing myself.

Maybe I have to lose the old me in order to find the new me?

I was going to title this piece, losing myself.
But I decided that's too negative and chose, finding myself instead.

Flipping the negative thought on its head.
That's something I would do, I'm so glad I haven't lost that part.

My positive outlook.
But the bits of me…. Where are they going and why?

Do they just rearrange themselves in my mind?
Perhaps it's all becoming too much?

Did I ever really know myself?
Perhaps it's time for self-discovery once I start listening to me.

But how do I do that? I feel as though I need to settle within myself.
Who do I feel are my people?

How do I do that with others if I can't do it for myself?
Recentering/reclaiming.

We don't learn from experiences.
We learn from how we process experiences.

Re-aiming.
Reframing.

Grace

That the heart can be both broken and full at the same time – this is grace.

Are You Ready

Like the smoke blowing the poison from your lungs that dissipates invisibly, with just the right amount of sunlight its presence abounds and surrounds. Suddenly it can no longer be unseen.

You know it's there.
As it's this feeling that steals bits of you in lonely moments of solitude.

It knows you seek this solitude for peace of mind, but it does not grant that to you, it so quietly sits in the background like a thick layer of mist.

Waiting to transform into all those nightmares sleeping in the back of your mind.

Made of insecurities and fear and doubt and pain.
It waits, not pretending to be kind......

Are you ready for it?

Carried Away

You place your troubles on the wings of the colorful birds you see gliding above as you stand by the edge of a peaceful cool river.

A peace you wish you could achieve.

You envision those troubles being carried away by the winged beauties so effortlessly.

You wonder how they can possibly be such a bother to you when they are so easily carried away by tiny fragile creatures?

I envy the bird that can just take flight and from their troubles just take off.

Rage and Hope

A rage is growing inside of me
from a bad seed planted long ago.
The kind of rage that leads to destruction,
its existence I despise.

So, I water its flames down with hope.
Hope that cascades like a waterfall working
to extinguish the raging flame completely, but
it always seems to endure and flicker back as a blaze.

Yet another seed grows deeper inside too. One tenderly
made from a mother's heart of love and
a father's soul of wisdom. You see,
hope has already been planted in me.

The question becomes
which seed
am I going to
nurture, water and feed?

Inescapable

I was a good girl.
Got good grades.
I shied away from the boys and their aggressive hands
or perhaps them from me.
Either way, I felt inept.
Confused.
So I just kept "busy".

My days were busy,
but my nights were filled too,
with more things to accomplish, more things to validate my existence.

I always kept moving,
and the dark shadow kept pursuing.
Because if I stopped,
the pain would come shooting.

I kept moving into adulthood.
Always did my best.
But my best didn't fill the unrest. Somehow those aggressive hands
would always find me.

Running from boredom,
into the army I enlisted.
To make the world a better place.
And I did in small ways.

When that wasn't enough to fill the familiar void, to the high
mountains of Central America I soared!
I used to think, I'll always
keep moving and the dark shadow
will likely keep pursuing.
I just won't stop and the
pain can't come shooting.

But I was lying to myself. No matter how far I kept moving, or how
much good I did, that dark shadow kept right on pursuing.

Then it dawned on me, I can't outrun myself. And you can't outrun yourself. Wherever I went, there I was. Wherever you go, there you will be.

Inescapable.

Let's be honest for one sec. I'm trying to find an escape from myself.

An outcast, a stranger in my own body.
Running alongside myself trying to hop on a rapidly moving train to catch a ride to some unknown destination.

As long as it isn't a place where I find my own company.
All the while through thick thigh high peanut butter. But staying "busy".

I catch up and see a snake wrapped around my neck methodically contracting as it winds.

Two bodies in a river wrestling. I'm on top of myself pushing me under the surface of the water wearing a most satisfying smile.

Gasping for sweet life-giving air.
Kneeling, my knees cut and bloodied, the sweat that runs down them gifts me an alleviating sting that I gladly accept.

Surrendering.

Last Star

It's easier to go to the last star in the galaxy than to reach the depths of my aching heart. Self-love is what I want, self-love is what I need. How to get there is the unknown, the murky in between.

Have you felt your emotions lately? I mean really felt them, not just been reactive to them?

Befriended them and asked them what it is they seek to tell you?

Or do you shove them deep inside where they can't be seen but tear you up internally?

A friend once said we are all made of stars that have come to consciousness. I say our feelings are as deep and complex as the space coloring in the black holes of the Universe.

"Interstellar"
Remember love was the answer in that story.

Mysterious.

Stay curious.

The Monster Within

I am sweet as sugar and soft as butter but do me wrong and I turn sour in a second.

My sugar turns to salt and my butter into lard.

Disturbed, the monster stirs.

Trying to be set free to wreak havoc on whatever lies in its path.

Ready to unleash its hurt from its past.
Not strong enough to just let things go,
not strong enough to just GO!

So, it stays inside wreaking havoc on me.
There it will stay for all eternity.
For I will not allow,
nor does it want,
to leave this home
from a soul
so sweet and soft.

Weapons

Weaponized words fired at me like bullets.
Bullets that ripped through the skin yet absorbed by the body without
a flinch. Stoic.

It's absurd as they leave me perturbed and on edge.
Maybe these are the kind of bullets I thought I deserved?

Weaponized weakness into your power.
Ready to have your cake and devour.
Like an animal, preyed upon while I was in my most vulnerable state.
Weaponized love for my soul to take.

Zero freedom,
on a leash,
so subtle and insidious, that it took years,
yet came on like a beast.

Weapons to break my kind heart and compassionate spirit,
caught in your love bomb,
exposed, now ready to explode.

YOU poured on the gas to light the wick.
So quick.
Gaslit.
Maybe I'll implode.

I've gone into survival mode.
Now I've caught on, ready to fight.
A switch has been flipped.
My bulletproof vest is fit and zipped.
Is it possible for us to recover
from something so sick?

Keep Fightin'

Feelin' a little bit inspired
although I'm tired
and it's hard to keep tryin',
pushin' farther and farther.

I woke up this morning,
not wanting to move,
but that inner self said you gots to prove
 ...that you can make it, take it,
it don't matter what they say.

It's that flame burnin' in you that eases your pain.
The world's not nice and won't help you, so, you gotta take that
flame, provoke it brighter and glow the beautiful that unfolds out of
your soul.

Give it some space to grow and set off
and when they trample on it,
tell 'em to fuck off.

You know your worth inside,
it doesn't matter how they stare or glare,
or set you up to fail.

You're stronger than that,
oh you know, it's true,
when you look in the mirror feel the pride swell and let it shine
through.

You put your war paint on day after day,
you think it makes you prettier,
well at least presentable to those who say, "You're ugly, not worth it
and full of shit".

Well until you can wash the paint off and clean yourself from the false
fix you will not be free and will always be
haunted by the shadow of insecurity.

What will it take to shake this inner demon?

A beer usually works, but that's the devil just scheming.

When that dark feeling is evoked, you've got to put your fighting gloves on and jab and poke until you hit something hard inside you that says "keep going, it's not worth it to run and hide."

Only you can erase that poor mentality and build up a stronger one that conquers all those painful ideals of mortality.

What I'm sayin' here is never give up, show a little attitude, and be tough.

For with your endurance, trust, and faith in yourself,
you'll find it's much easier on this world's stage and within this script of life itself.

Float Through the Storm with Me

You gotta swim through the darkness
to get to the other side of it.

Notice how I didn't say sit in it.
You can't dwell or it will eat…... you…... alive.

Not only will it dim your light, but it will snuff it out for good.
When you swim, you bob and weave through the highs and lows of the tide. You didn't create the waves but must learn to navigate them, learn how to ride.

They smack you in the face and it hurts like hell, FEEL IT, and roll on.
Over and over again likely for all of this human life.

It's okay to tread water when you feel you are using every ounce of energy you have just to keep your head above water.

Don't forget to ask for your life vest every now and then when you need it. But you MUST feel it, accept it, and keep up the fight.

If you need to, call on me, I can make a pretty good life preserver. I'd love to just sit and float through the storm with you.

Brown Eyes

I was tucking my 9-year-old into bed. I was hugging her in front of me, her little head just below mine. Close enough where I could squeeze my arms around hers in a bear hug and give her a kiss. She suddenly looked up at me with her big, gorgeous saucer-like brown eyes and examined my face for what seemed like a full minute then landing ultimately on my eyes locking her gaze there. I just watched and waited patiently to hear what was on her mind.

Then she said randomly out of the blue, "You really are beautiful." I was overcome. Overcome with a feeling of love and with a feeling of me in her words. Little me, peering back at me, trying to tell me I was beautiful. Trying to convince me once and for all. The universe was using her as a conduit for my healing. I thought, maybe it thinks I will listen to my own words? Tears began to stream down my face. "Thank you, sweetie, you are even more," is how I responded. She asked, "Why are you crying? You don't hear that very often do you?" I told her they were happy tears. She seemed content.

Now if only I could believe her.

Slowly, I think I do.

Acknowledging that sometimes, I do feel beautiful.

The Thaw

As the snow starts to thaw and the season begins to break,
so does my heart from its solitary ache.

The sun warms the ice around my cold exterior,
to reveal the special inside built of gold interior.

I must let it shine bright and not be caught below the callous,
for it has good to do in this world that is as delicate as the flower's chalice.

Part III: The Healing

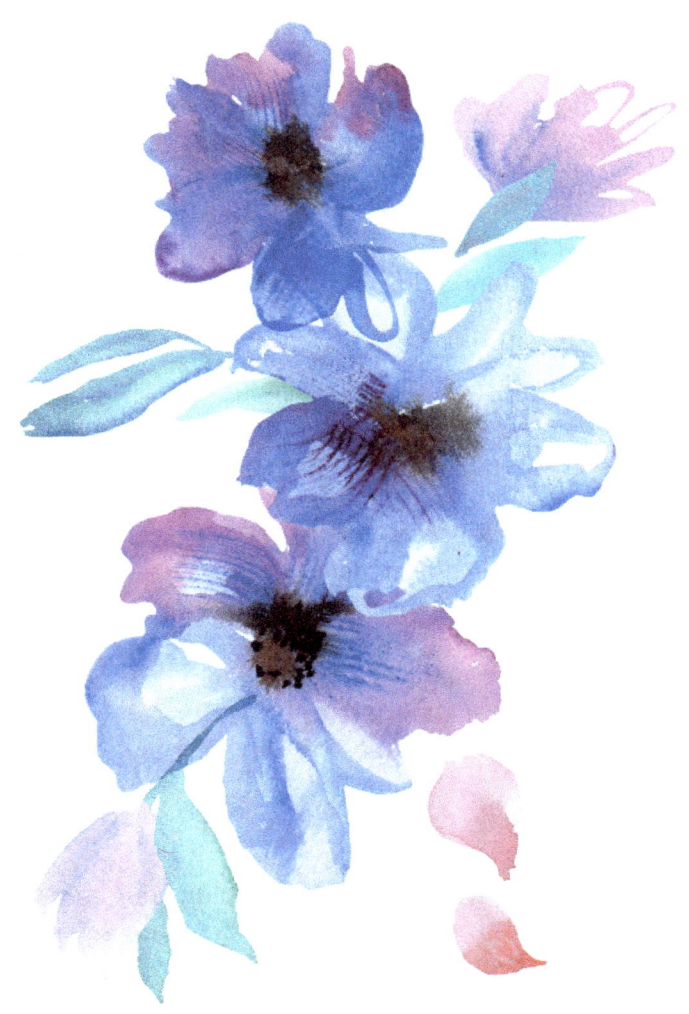

What If You Didn't Know the Sun?

It's a time so dark you can't even see your hand in front of your face. There's a chill that goes deep into the center of your bones and settles there unwavering accompanied by an empty darkness that stays for what feels like eternity.
Seconds tick by ever so slowly and you begin to wonder when you'll ever feel some relief. You fight blindly and cold and alone with no sense of control. Indefinitely.

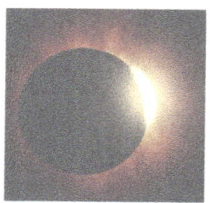

Out of nowhere something interrupts the darkness and chill, an intervention outside of your realm of understanding.
Light peeks its head over the ridge of eternity. You feel instant relief that melts the chill, eases aching bones, and provides peace and warmth.

Sudden, beautiful clarity!
Not only do you see your hand in front of your face but the world in all its shades of color.

> We need the darkness; without it, we would not know the sun or warmth or peace.
> Embrace them both.

As is within us, when we go through chaotic lonely dark times.
Allow, no...... invite the stranger darkness to have its stay within you. Let it sit with you. For if not, it will keep on knocking and visiting as it pleases.
Lurking.

> If you pull the shades in isolation, plug your ears to deafen its call, hide under the covers in an effort to be undiscovered, and ignore it to soften its blow, then you will not come to know the sun.
> Listen to what the unknown is whispering to you as it has a message for you to unwind.

Image from Microsoft Word 2010

Then look inside for resolution as nobody and nothing else can get it to go away except you.
It's for you to find.

> Be vigilant for the great interrupter. Have faith it will manifest just as the sun did. You did not know the sun but when it appeared
> you understood.

The same will occur and will be catered to *YOUR* unique unknown.
It will be okay.
Be brave and be strong.

> Let it stay so that it will leave.
> Its arrival is always unknown and chaotic, but its exit, its exit you not only control, but create.
> Embrace it with open arms so that it will leave
> and then,
> prepare to know your sun.

Invisible Child

She waits in silence as you grow and mature.
She waits in silence hoping you'll pay attention to her.
Crying inside and observing you as you leave her forgotten.
She observes you staying busy,
achieving more,
pushing yourself more, more, and even more……
yet pushing her deeper into the darkness within.

It's almost as if you believe that if a hint of her weakness shows
it's some sort of sin.
Growing lonelier by the day
she wonders if you'll ever set her free, ever take her out of her misery.

Not causing trouble,
perhaps a little distress,
but by and large trapped quietly at your heart's depth.

She is the little one looking to feel accepted.
So vulnerable,
she is the little one no longer wanting to feel rejected.

She is the little one who tries and tries
to be so good.
She is the little one who wishes you understood.

Understood……
that your worth does not come from the things you accomplish.
Your worth doesn't come from pleasing others in a world that is so selfish.

It comes just from you being you
and you believing that to be true.
So, open your eyes if you are willing,
you see,
open your arms to her and embrace her,
hold her close for all eternity.

For when this child is no longer invisible and is not diminished
but is loved and cherished…...
she will allow you to relinquish all your powerful parts of which have
been banished.

You hold the key,
now unlock your heart,
and set yourself free.

But give your invisible child the grace to slowly rise in her power
and be finally seen.

Let her walk out with pride ever so gently.

Humanity

Eyes closed, feel the warmth of the sun.
A tear of mixed emotion rolls down an indifferent face, leaving a shiny path on its way down.
The most beautiful orange and red sunset glows softly as it peers through the trees. It nods a gentle good night,
a reminder that we are not in control.

We fail to see.
See through the thick skulls and thin skin we have created for ourselves. We hoard and try to control at the cost of the collective. We fail to compromise and we steal from the earth for our own convenience and power.
We take and use until there is no more.

At... what... Cost?
Are the riches of Mother Earth without limit... or have we reached ours?
A *self-inflicted* checkmate.

It is said that under the pressure of extraordinary circumstances new outcomes arise.
We are part of a process; we are setting just as surely as the sun does daily.

Yet, we evolve.
Intertwined, you and me, and everything else that ever existed. These days I feel closer to the beauty of the setting sun than the indignity of being human.
The rivers and seas are her veins, and the trees are her lungs.

So, a tear flows... not of sadness.
A formulation, a numbing concoction of human emotion,
and it just is. Feel, be still......
it doesn't die there. At the confluence of humanity and spirituality there is appreciation and hope.

Appreciation in the unity of being part of something much greater where perhaps the outcome is already written with purpose. Gratitude in each setting sun and each nod into the bold bright night.

Hope that the universe still has many more nods in store for the human spirit. Hope that we will learn.

Let Father Time be gracious.
It is a certainty that even after we have fulfilled our flawed roles on Mother Earth, she will surely live on.

We will live on too.

Seas of Life

World in chaos, chaos in the world spiraling like a torpedo to what seems to be the darkest hearts of humanity....
Darkness doesn't stay, not forever.

Where there's an up there's a down, an in and an out, a smile and a frown. An action and opposite reaction. Newton's third law, this we can count on.

Then does this mean there is no reality;
it's just our vantage point depending on where we live, who we know, or what we believe?

I take advantage of what I see, I seize the day, or do I just say I do? Is that my will or wish rather than true carpe diem?

O captain, my captain, will you captain my ship? The ship riding through the stormy seas of time?

The stormy seas of the darkest of hearts make it easy to lose a sense of direction. Life isn't for the faint of heart, it gives and takes and breaks us down like powerful waves breaking on the rocks of the deep and bold blue.

But all the while without us knowing it shapes us and sharpens us. Then there's calm again and you take a moment to view the reflection peering back in the still, cool water.

Silence surrounds. Do you recognize that face and see how it's weathered through the sands of time?

Do you appreciate and cherish each scar and freckle and line that's been created as a path to the unique maze of you?

Do you see the beauty others see in you? Do others see the beauty you see in them?

Whispers blow through, wondering if you share that with them and if you are listening.

Hang on and hang in for the deepest hearts of darkness there is light.

We must ride each storm and embrace its own unique challenges. Choose your ship and your crew wisely. If one ship doesn't work out, then repair or replace or try another for good fit but sail on and keep searching for that lighthouse through the seas of life.

It's there, closer than you think.

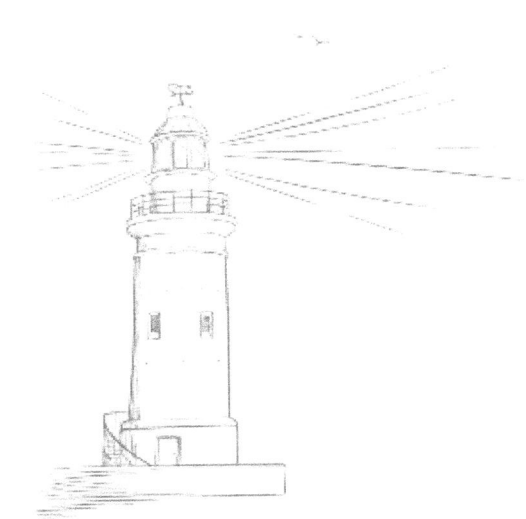

Journey

Imagine stepping down from the train onto the platform so
deliberately like a hammer onto a nail symbolizes the job is done.

Courageously take a deep breath of cool fresh air and turn your face up towards the sky,
feel the warmth of the sun's rays.
Your cheeks begin to feel rosy.

The smell of the new blossoms in the air persuades you this is indeed a fresh start along with the spring.

When soul and nature and humanity collide,
if only for a split second,
we move in unison…..
as one,
and there is CERTAIN tranquility.

A tranquility that rejuvenates.

Let us refuel for the next journey ahead.

Love

The felty softness of leaves tickling the bottom of my fingertips as they slip through my hand as I stroll by.

The smell of wild wet flowers and plants sprinkled along the bumpy and winding path along the river.

The sensation of the breeze whispering through the tiny hairs on my face and filling my lungs with the wholeness of life.

Present and precious moments where awareness and appreciation merge.

A higher level. One that rises above the distraction of the toxic.

Living in that space, is a sense of euphoria and peace.

Hoping words will capture the majesty.
As I peer into the eyes of my loved ones, I reflect on the hard road traveled to be in the current moment.
A road that meant self-sacrifice and compromise and patience.

We are so quick to quit when things are hard.
A few live with the pain and work toward shared understanding and acceptance of people for who they are.

It's slowly building love, love isn't just here for the taking,
it's here for the creating, it's here for the building. Taking chances, risking your heart along the way.

The sensation described above is love in its fullest sense.
Love only felt through living imperfect lives with imperfect beings.

Love lives longer than we ever will, when felt, bottle it up, and hold it close to the soul.

Bucket Full of Tears

Tears that stream so often and so profusely.
Each tear represents my love for you.

A love that stems from the deepest parts of my being.
Tears for every memory we've made.
Tears for every giggle we ever exchanged.
Tears for every big sister moment and karaoke song we sang.
Tears for every dance floor we opened.
Tears for every night we closed.
I do not think the tears will ever stop flowing for someone who is so worthy of knowing.

A bucket of sad tears for you are slowly fading away.
A bucket full of happy tears for all you have given and for how brightly you shine. It won't be easy to dim your light.

I won't waste the time we have left crying over what could have been.

I will use the time to soak every minute in.

My tears have filled a bucket.
And if each tear represents my love for you,
let's call it a big bucket of love.

That is all I have ever had
and all I will ever have for you.
If I've learned anything from you,
it's to live life to the max each and every day.

Real tears and metaphorical tears, that tear at my soul in waves.
Like a piece of my being slowly being peeled away in a painful slow burn.
I wonder if I pour my bucket of love tears on top of my chest it will extinguish the burn in my heart?

While the physical part may be fading, the spirit and essence of your beautiful soul will forever remain.

The brightest star in the sky.
Lighting my path, reminding me to keep moving forward in my truth.

Making me laugh with you, and as I laugh, I see that big, gorgeous smile of yours shining through.

Age Demented

Is age a measure of life in time
or
a measure of growth in life?

Worn and weathered we were supposed to be together.
Cracking jokes and up to mischief.
Spontaneous and fun,
always on the run.

I wanted to grow old with you
and grow wise.
But father time has something else up his sleeve.
He might make you leave
sooner than we
believed.

Your brain is no longer aging normally.
Accelerated aging.
Curious.
Polluted by something so
mysterious.

I soak up these moments we have together today
and try to trap them in my memory
like how a sponge absorbs spilled coffee rolling
astray.

Tomorrow, I want to remember
yesterday.
Seared there with care,
but free enough to breathe
and move with the
air.

Our time is growing grander and grander,
expanding as we soak up experiences
together.

I want to freeze our sponges and keep them close.
That way time will be frozen there
forever.

But the years seem as though they are speeding up
and I'm losing time as they race on by.
Sometimes it feels like precious time wasted with
how I fill it with meaningless tasks.

All I ask is that your age slows down and you
outlast
your doctor's life
forecast.

Forgive me for wasting time on the meaningless
fluff,
it's just stuff
to fill the extra space in between for the rest of
us.
Extra isn't a luxury for you to mess with
and that puts it into
perspective.

Sometimes it feels like you're aging in reverse.
Childlike with joyful glee.
Maintaining your sense of humor,
trying your best to be
carefree.

Maybe that's what our brains do with your
condition,
grow backwards
rapidly.
If that's the case could you allow your heart to
take over so you'll never forget
me?
Or never forget us
or what together as a family
means?

As you make your long walk home, know that I'm
always here with you
walking beside you
down that long path
in whatever way your body chooses to
sidetrack.

Besides, your body is just a vessel and we're really
only speaking of life in terms of its bodily
resistance,
not your continued
<u>FULL</u> existence.
In your next form, I wonder if age is even a thing
at all?

When you get there,
please wait for me.
If I get there first,
I'll have your space reserved
next to me,
pausing patiently,
between worlds.

Age is just an evolution of time.
A number that eventually ceases to climb.
The resolution of bodily life.

Extraordinary

I invite you to be dazzled by the ordinary. Ordinary is extraordinary.
The sounds of croaking frogs in the distance are peaceful sounds to my child lying in bed at night.
Extraordinary.

A cloud weighs thousands of pounds yet can effortlessly just float on by in the sky.
Extraordinary.

The sun can shine, and the rain is able to pour simultaneously.
Extraordinary.

A child's innocent forwardness can be the piercing words of honesty we need to hear at just the right moment in the gentlest way possible.
Extraordinary.

Our bodies and hearts and minds grow without making a sound loud enough to the naked ear.
Extraordinary.

Accept the invitation.

Swept Away

I close my eyes so gently and all I hear is the wind blowing softly through the trees.

The birds, children playing, and roosters are just background music.

My attention is focused on the wind's song.

I lose myself in it.

With my eyes closed I feel as if I'm home in Minnesota.

The wind holds the same tune no matter where I am.

I fall back home as I listen to the breeze blowing through the trees and across my body.

I am swept away to another land,
as I lay listening to the same song of the wind in this strange and foreign one,
it doesn't seem that foreign.

Molded Clay

We may not have chosen the life
given to us which has molded and shaped us, but
we can choose to change it.

Deciding to invest in ourselves and put
in the hard work to deal with and confront
hardship so that we mold and change ourselves
towards the direction we want to go.

Instead of having been molded, we
mold ourselves into our next best.

Doing nothing isn't an option.

We manifest.

Clouds

Bending and forming,
    changing with each new season.

Slowly at first
and then,

        in an instant

                towards the end,

                      so it is in life.

                The present seems long,
                    the past,
                  just yesterday.

      And tomorrow?

I wonder what it will have in store.

          A mystery for us to solve evermore.

Soaked Through

The sun's rays soaked through my skin and eased my every muscle,
until they were so relaxed,
they melted into the earth.

I melted into the earth and became one with it.
The sense of balance and tranquility
made me never want to leave.

It was like a state of ecstasy given by a drug.
No cares, no problems,
No one's opinions affecting my life.

Just the earth and me finally together again.
Together making harmonious songs and I,
so calm that I was the earth,
just like the beginning,
and the earth was me.

Fear or Courage

At first,
I was afraid of thunderstorms,
but now I've come to love their controlled and beautiful chaos that lights up the sky and how they cathartically weep once they've worked through the tumult.

I used to be afraid to give speeches,
now I've learned to love how words, tone, and inflection can be used as an art to captivate a crowd
and unveil one's heart.

I had a fear of traveling alone,
but now I love the adventure of meeting new people and places and pushing through vulnerability and
finding strength on the other side.

I used to fear falling in love, now I've learned to
love the risk of giving your all, your entirety to someone/something else.

If everything I once feared I've learned to love,
maybe I should do more of the things I fear?
The opposite of fear is courage,
courage to do that which you fear is one of the most priceless gifts in the world.

The question is, what is stronger in you?
<u>Fear</u> or <u>courage</u>?

Make a Splash

Minty freshness, the gum saturates my mouth.
Its flavor jumps off of my taste buds just like the frogs around me leaping from the tall wet grass by the river to splash into the clear warm water.

Splash, I like that word. Did you make a splash today? Did you make today count?

Never content with the mundane, must keep pushing the envelope so that we aren't enveloped by the negativity that life brings.

So bring life!

There's so much tranquility and majesty to behold.
I hold onto the simple as there lies the special.

The beauty,
unique.
Longing for peace.
Longing for subtlety.

The subtle touch of arms that wrap around me like a warm blanket on a cold day, suspended there, like the cloud that blows out from the lungs in cool air.

Suspended in the comfort of an abundance of love that never fades.

To be able to sink into someone's arms for an unknown amount of time and just melt into them.

Everything fades though, doesn't it?

Love, memories, life.
In a second it can go….. its end date we are not to know.

Make a splash as we don't know how long it will last.

There is something to be said for you only live once.

We humans are to live in the now.

It's how we're constructed.

How do YOU make a splash?

Or do you choose to make waves instead?

Ignited by the Light

Ignited by the light, ready to fight!

Until night comes and the demons take hold. Be bold. Be strong. Let the momentum take hold.

Resist the negative. Be persistent and deliberate.

Do not deliberate on that which is uncertain, rely on your intuition and move forward. Fake it until you make it, until you reach the destination.

Your choice.

You do have a voice worthy of being heard. Beyond the limiting voice in your head, so absurd.

This work is for all of us. Take hold and take flight. Ignited by the light within that God so graciously filled, don't allow it to dim.

Beautiful Child

Oh, beautiful child of mine, your name is the lyric of my heart.

> I look at you and see the magic of the world in your eyes.

Your giggle echoes the innocence of a time where I appreciated everything for what it was. It brings back fond memories of the simple joys of life.

> Days letting the sun shine bright on my face without worrying about sunscreen.

A time where I ran free and felt the grass squish between my toes, staining my feet, not worrying about ticks and germs and disease.

> A simpler time or at least I thought.

My friends were my neighbors, and my neighbors were my friends. I didn't search for them on social media. I knew their home telephone numbers by heart.

> A time where we created worlds with our imagination with the help of sticks and rocks and trees and lakes and dirt for hours on end.

Hours.........until you could see the day nodding good evening with the gentle setting of the sun and a mother's voice in the distance hollering that dinner was ready.

> Baby boy and girl of mine thank you for reigniting this profound source of joy I had forgotten to flex.

Your name is the lyric of my heart, and you light the path where I experience life anew. I am reinvigorated by the lessons of life you teach and of which I am humbled.

Mother

A simple word for a complex role.
Being Mom is epic, such an important duty.
Mama, the sweetest word to hear now that I am one.
To be one is to appreciate one…. on a whole other level.
The wisdom that comes with age and experience, or maybe not even wisdom but perspective, and even more so appreciation, makes me see you with fresh eyes and even more admiration as the years pass by.

Madre so integral, so key, so constant.
I reflect on you my Mama and am so filled with love. So simple, so complex, so important. So, mine. I love you and thank you for being my Mama. Now Grandma too.

Grand indeed, beyond expectation.

Baby Breath

The sweet sound of your little baby breath upon the pillow calms my nerves from a stressful day full of corporate America's empty and short-term promises. You fill me with the long-term promise of love.

Your smile beams with sunshine that fills my world and lifts my soul.

Your laughter is music to my ears that brushes darkness away.

The pitter pat of your little feet echoes into the sweetest of my dreams.

Your cries and squeaks remind me of the precious and fragile beings of humanity we are.

My heart aches from top to bottom and all the way to its core with a love so grand it cannot be contained. An aching I'm so fortunate to have.

It spills out of me through so many tears of love and joy it hurts. I could produce a river with these tears.

What a beautiful gift which has been given to us. A gift which these mere mortal English words attempt to accurately describe, yet still fall short. It's the kind of love that is so powerful it permeates through me and fills my world, perhaps even yours.

My cup indeed runneth over; until this instant I don't know that I completely understood what that meant. The greatest sense of gratitude.

It is impossible to describe the sheer and utter beauty. All I can do is surrender to the awesome filled wonder of it all.

Skeleton Key

Perhaps we are unable to unlock the opportunity to heal because we are using the same old key, just as key styles have changed, so have we.

The skeleton key that opened the door before is now a flat piece of charged plastic that we simply wave across a door to unlock it and get in.

Perhaps try another key to unlock your potential.

You have nothing to lose, but to be stuck behind the same closed door. You will never know until you garner the courage to try.

Fire Crackling Rose

She is like wildfire.

Fire crackling echoes of light into the darkness of night.
The darkness tries to diminish her flame, hugging her with its uninvited and overreaching shadow.

Slow and stealth like shadow, she didn't know you were there, sucking and draining the oxygen from her light.

Did you think she would let you prevail? She sneaks her space and when the time is right, she knows, oh she knows...that's when her soul will take flight.

The embers are reassembling. They are dim but don't be fooled, these embers are ready for fresh wind to refuel.
She knows with each breath, be it small, be it shallow, she's alive and building her strength for battle.

Her specs of beautiful red orange float through the vast sky, gliding in freedom, waiting to rekindle new life.
We admire the beauty of those embers and yearn to be close to their warmth.

Silently we wait with heart filled anticipation knowing it won't be long before we see a rose-colored horizon.
She's like wildfire, crackling echoes of delight filling the world with warmth, love, and light.

Try to catch an ember, if you dare, and be ready to feel your world be lifted from despair.

Fire crackling embers filling the world with delight and all those who capture a piece with love, happiness and hope ready to ignite!

The Light

It's like there was this light in my life as I was a child growing up, even into adolescence and young adulthood.

That's why I never knew I lived in so much darkness before.
You were my light. You kept me light.

I thank the universe,
I think your light was meant for me.

Maybe I recognized the light in you that shines so bright as a beam or spotlight guiding a path and getting me through.

Maybe you brought my strengths towards that spotlight drawing them out,
helping me keep going without even knowing it.

Maybe it was a little bit of both,
either way,
you are a gift.

As I Wander, I Wonder

As I wonder, I wander.

Why was I spared?
What does God have in store for me?
What purpose, I've always wondered, there surely must be.
I want to be an agent of good.
Impactful positivity.

Then it dawned on me, maybe I am simply a testimony of hope, love, and God's incredible power.
People used to approach me and ask,
"Were you that baby who was so sick? We prayed so hard for you."

Often strangers would say this to me growing up and I found it annoying as that wasn't the way I wanted to be known.

I wanted them to know me.

But I see now that was a very childish and selfish way to look at that. Now that I am older, and have a deeper understanding, I see the beauty of being used as a vessel of hope.

I used to ask God what more he wanted me to do. But now I see that I've fulfilled some of that purpose.

What more was I searching to be?
Perhaps I've fulfilled my destiny.

What's Your Sunshine?

Sometimes the only thing
standing in the way of acceptance
is yourself.

I know now the only thing getting in my way
is me.

Such vulnerability.
To realize this truth,
at the core, is freeing…... yet,
the shadow looms.

We are not always to understand
but accept and learn to live
with what is.

It helps to choose to
stand in the sunshine.

What's your sunshine?

Nature's Music

There is music in nature.

To be human in a moment
is to allow yourself to experience
all the nuances.

All senses and seasons work in harmony.

Fall leaves floating to the ground
sing of a season setting to rest,
dormant, before that
of rejuvenation and regeneration.

Nature shines so bright in summer that it even needs to pull back and reset to emerge as bright again.

As it is with us, seasons of brightness
and seasons of rejuvenation.

We ought to let nature take the lead and listen to her
rather than the expectations placed upon us
by ourselves and other humans.

I am convinced answers in life are all found in nature
if we pay attention to it.
If not answers, at least lessons.

Look to nature.

Go ahead, ask our Mother Earth.

Fire, Water, Wind, and Earth

I am fire, water and wind and earth. Made of the earth and therefore belong. Fire in my heart that so deeply feels in order to heal. Water pulsating through my veins keeps me running as the rivers flow. Wind behind my back, that pushes me so.

That same wind paradoxically so soft it tickles my soul as over my bare skin it gently floats across.

Grounded in fire and water, wind and earth. Grateful for their offerings of which I gladly accept. Even when the wind turns into a violent storm, it has a purpose and something to share that I best not neglect, I'll sit with it until it passes, waiting to intercept the message. Waiting for when it's ready to whisper gently in my ear all that it has to reveal.

But when the flame in my heart turns to fire and my wind sets it ablaze, I'll need to remember all that I am to get me through the haze. Waiting in the wings, water is there, ready to extinguish the churn and burn residing in despair. Yet, Mother Earth knows and she's prepared to console by having me plant new roots to foster rebirth.

I am fire and water and wind and earth. I breathe in with purpose and powerful intent. The breeze subtly stokes the dimming fire in my heart making it braver, stronger, more extraordinarily able to give and receive grace and feel content.

Game of Chess

Sometimes I'm the pawn, sometimes the knight,
sometimes the rook or the bishop depending on who's needed in strife.

Waiting for the time,
a time when the timing is right.

A time to identify, encapsulate and be the Queen I'm meant to be.

Even if that means, especially if that means, I'm the Queen of the best in me.

The Queen of my OWN heart.

For now, I'll be a good knight, I've got the Queen's back,
but strategically I'm continuing the inner fight until I prevail, and she reigns over all who hail.

And if I fail there's always another try, a chance to play a new role to get to where I want or need to go.

The key to opening the Queen's heart is never giving up and learning with each fresh start.

Insignificant Significance

Changed forever by the smallness.
The big changes didn't move the dial.
In small subtle moves there is big progress.
It's the seemingly insignificant routine that
turns into something significant over time.

Creation is Quiet

We don't hear our wounds healing, but we feel them and even see them heal.

We don't hear ourselves growing, but we feel and see our growth.

We don't hear our teeth straightening under the metal in our mouths, but we feel and see when they are straightened.

We don't hear our bodies resting, but we feel and see the difference in the morning.

We don't hear babies growing in the uterus, but we feel them move.

We don't hear our spirits lifting, but we feel it.

We don't hear peace in our hearts, but we feel it.

We don't hear our thoughts literally, but the impact of them is beyond measure.

Just because we don't hear them though, doesn't mean they don't make a sound.

Some things created are better left in the quiet. So unspeakable, they are not worthy of being heard.

Leave those things there, focus on the beautiful quiet creations and bring those to consciousness.

Shadows

The candle
glows and creates a shadow
on the corner of the wall.

The shadow's mystery lures us in
for it does not take up space,
yet we can see it and it remains.

Like a whisper of encouragement to a child
mustering up the confidence
to face their fears.

A whisper that ignites the hope of possibility.

Possibility creates dreams and dreams are life itself.

Without dreams what are we?

Just passing through space and time
floating like limbs of a dandelion in the breeze.

So, we dare to reach to the furthest corners of our imaginations.
Some say our society is hollow, shallow, void, empty.

The people who believe in this country dream of a place of possibility,
a place of hope, and a place of good.

We dreamers will dream on and collectively whisper into each other's
ears,
"Get up and face your fears."

When the corners feel as though they are caving in,
we must remember they are figments.

For in that space of our imaginations,
the space where dreams come from,
corners do not exist.

My hand touches the shadow on the wall as a reminder it remains.
We must come out from under the shade.

My voice breaks the silence of complicity to create
space and growth and room for others
to fulfill their wildest dreams in a country full of possibility.

For those without a voice have always been here enduring through the silent shadows carrying U.S. forward.

Shadows created by us; yet, unobserved and denied by U.S.

They are the light; they are the strong underestimated of our past and the passageway to our bright future where, together, shadows fade.

Walk Into Your Joy

I walked a path today.
It was a path created by my mind.
It took me to all the places I needed to go.
Carved of golden bricks that brilliantly radiated light.

I felt like Dorothy in *The Wizard of Oz*. I wondered if I clicked my heels together and chanted, "There's no place like home" three times I'd be whisked back to my home. There truly is no place like it with its intimate comfort and welcome.

And although I find truth in that statement, this path was about light and love and something else entirely.

Finding, or perhaps recognizing that which makes us light up with joy out in the world. All roads lead to somewhere, perhaps it meant being able to feel at home within myself?

Like, in *The Alchemist*, sometimes we need to venture away from home to be able to see and find it. Or perhaps away from ourselves? As Santiago journeyed through Egypt and back to Spain to create or maybe even be able to see his joy shining back at him.

As the road twisted and turned beneath my feet, I tripped on the uneven bricks, yet the smile on my face grew and grew. Like when the Grinch's heart finally melted in the end and he found his joy and the heart in his chest pounding through.

As I walked, I saw to my right rows of gorgeous blue, purple, and yellow flowers sprinkled over a hill of deep green grass. My nostrils could sense the faint sweet flowery fragrance as I turned my head to the other side. To my left, I heard splashing and saw two silver dolphins playing in the deep turquoise sea with their elegance and playful sass.

With light still radiating up through my feet I felt a brisk air sweep across my face and it rejuvenated my pace and gait.

Then I saw them, my baby boy and girl, and I watched as they grew. The greatest source of my joy. The unconditional love, the connection that's so strong. It's so incredibly stunning.

Then I looked at my friends and family and beamed with joy for the uniqueness and special contributions they make to the family and world just by being in it as themselves.
The rainbows and flowers and gold and riches along the way of my path meant nothing alone.

Only when shared did I find my joy and feel most alive. Only when shared will I be able to find myself and feel at home.
As such, I share this with you.

Walk, run, then collide into your joy.

I Am Not My Darkness

I am not my darkness.
I radiate light that's just temporarily covered like an eclipse.

I keep saying those words over and over as the stormy clouds swirl in my head like a tsunami about to hit.

I gaze at a candle and its tiny flicker. It's as if it's pointing at me with a finger then curling it back towards itself, inviting me to come closer to learn how to ignite my flame again.

My gaze turns into longing.

Longing to feel my life-giving force, my energy to infuse love and positivity in the world. Longing and waiting without judgement, albeit painstakingly.

Hoping, wishing, cradling my flame, protecting its light so that when I'm ready, it'll burn so bright that all I am near will be left with a feeling of unconditional warmth. Like an embrace that wraps them with such a force of life that they will never be able to escape.

I am not my darkness.

Rise Like the Sun

Healing is like a sunrise. A slow gradual rising full of intention and steady pursuit. Movements so slow and subtle that you don't realize until you, like the sun, have risen.

Blink, and miss the opportunity to see it. Numb it out and miss the opportunity to feel it.

Lucky for us there's another sunrise tomorrow. Another chance to feel and melt away our sorrow.

Heal steadily and with grace as it makes the burn less intense. Offer the worries of your own incompetence at the forefront, front and center.

Go ahead, raise it up, as that way, it will be the first to burn and you will learn and feel self-worth. Then you will see how far you have risen, no longer looking back, but forward in solidarity and without self-division.

Resilience

As much as I'd like there to be a beginning, middle, and an end for us, true healing doesn't work like that.

It's important to acknowledge that.

It's not linear.

It is a process,
a lifelong journey.

Just when you think it's gone and vanished for good, it's there again, peering back at you.

Never give up. That's why we need each other from which to ground and connect through the toughest times.

For every setback, there's another great comeback.
Resilience is what we need to find and build together.

Wish for You

I want you to feel love.

The kind of love you feel when someone is admiring you while you sleep.

You know the one,
when they are looking and you're wide awake,
but you don't open your eyes because you're feelin' the love and you know that they don't know you're awake, soaking it all in.

That's the love I wish for you to feel.

You deserve to feel adored.

Pockets of Love

I put your love in my pocket,
then it spilled over and filled two.

It just kept overflowing and now I have no more pockets left to fill
with all of this love from you.

So, I'll take it to my heart and bury it firmly there.

Where I intently will it to transform into self-love so that emptiness
will not prevail.

The Final Frontier

The final frontier is that of our own potential.

If only we are brave enough to adventure.

To search, encounter, and discover our souls.

Then share them with others and let the power take hold.

Layered love and acceptance to behold.

How far are you willing to go?

Be brave,

Be bold!

Me vs. Me

Float like a butterfly and sting like a bee. Said by the strong and relentless Muhammad Ali.

I float in and out of consciousness living partly in my head. Creating stories in my mind that bob and weave with the truth as they thread.

Needling me through dark tunnels of my past,
fighting against invisible ghosts in some sort of hypnotizing trance.

Until I find myself completely sewn in,
like into a spider's web,
I'm cocooned within the woven matrix of the brain inside my aching head.

I wrack that brain day after day,
but I'm left marooned and unable to explain.

That this spell I'm under
feels like my own self-inflicted hell.
A face off
against myself.

I'm ready to face that place
where my demons dwell.

I can't explain or exactly tell
but blow after blow
the deeper I go,
I gain ground
as my thoughts swirl and whirl
as I twirl and dance with these old tropes.

Up against the ropes,
my heart feels the dings,
but the sound of the bell
sparks my inner strength within and with each ring.

It's an awakening!
A bell full of alarm
I begin to conceive
I begin to believe
a deeper level of meaning
of consciousness
a more thorough understanding.

Round after round I zig and zag
floating with my stinger
flying high
ready to throw a zinger.

My resolve does not bend.
I do not break.
My mind weaves new tunnels
away from the ghosts who try my soul to take.

Untethered from those woven ropes
that tie me up in knots,
as long as I'm still tied to hope
all is not lost.

I let out my battle cry and punch through the pain,
knowing with every blow delivered
I have my entire self to gain.

Now unleashed from pieces spoiled and soured.
I'm generating new life,
that's bold and brave
is fulfilled and empowered, embracing all of that hidden superpower.

I shed self-limiting layers
and lift myself from the confusing cocoon of erroneous beliefs and behaviors.

I fly like a beautiful butterfly and sting like a determined bee. I am as strong and as relentless in my healing as the late great Muhammad Ali.

I am great too,
the great epitome,

of a true story worthy of retelling.

The Battle of Me vs. Me.

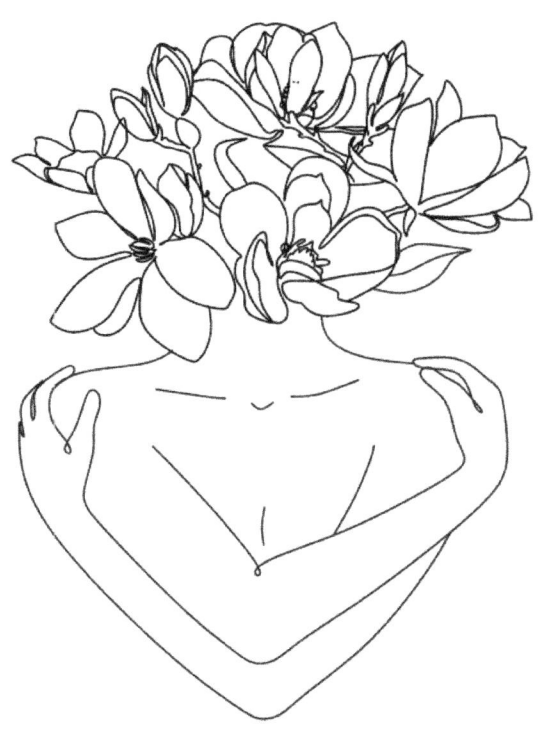

Acknowledgements

This collection of poetry wouldn't have come together without so many incredible people. I thank Krista Lindquist and Nicole Washburn, authors, coaches, and co-creators of *Opening the Channel to Write Your Story* for believing and diving into the unknown channel of this work with me. Your insight was powerful and unwavering, always leaving me with positive energy with every interaction. I can feel that you are truly in it to help people. Seeing your vision come to life has been inspiring.

To Marnie Harper, for encouraging me to write and pour it out so I could make sense of it all and for supporting me even when it was difficult. Your patience, knowledge, and kindness are so impactful.

I have heartfelt gratitude for my wonderful family and friends for being my touchstones and grounding me in this life. Each of you has a piece of my heart and when put together, you fill it entirely. Thank you for always loving me and accepting me as I am through my ups and downs; you are my light. I give thanks to my parents for their steadfast love and unwavering support that has created and continues to nurture me into the strong person that I am today.

To my dear friend Lynn Koski for your beautiful artwork on the front and back covers. Your paintings, wire sculptures, and other art are so deeply profound; it is such a gift to see our young scheming and dreaming come to life! I encourage everyone to contact you to view this brilliance at @lynnkoski_art.

To Mary Delorié, you have helped shape the best parts of me. You literally ARE *my* "Fire Crackling Rose" and "The Light." 💜

Lastly, to my readers, I hope you felt something deeply in this work and were able to connect through art and self-expression. Now go, share your light with the world! That is why we are here, to nurture growth and foster healing and connection wherever we can. Thank you for connecting with me by reading this work. I am forever grateful.

Inspired By...

You may have recognized and resonated with my use of familiar tunes, words, and movies throughout this collection, and I hope this allowed you to relate more deeply and remember the impact of these references in your own life.

I thank and honor the following works and artists for inspiring my own lyrics of the heart...

Self
"uninvited, not allowed,"
Morrisette, Alanis, "Uninvited." From the Album "City of Angels, Music from the Motion Picture", Producers Cavallo, Rob, Morrisette, Alanis, Label Maverick, February 24th, 1998.

Nothing Is Something
"let it go, let it go, just be one with the wind and sky,"
Lopez, Robert Joseph, and Anderson, Kristen Jane. Artist Menzel, Idina, "Let It Go." Soundtrack From the Original Motion Picture "Frozen", Disney, October 21, 2013.

Soft Heart
"killing me softly,"
Fox, Charles, Gimbel, Norman, and Lieberman, Lori. Producers The Fugees, Singer Hill, Loren, "Killing Me Softly." From the Album "The Score", Rough House, Columbia, May 27th, 1996.

Pieces
"The Truman Show"
Niccol, Andrew. Producers Ruden, Scott, Niccol, Andrew, Feldman, Edward S., Schroeder, Adam, "The Truman Show" Starring Carrey, Jim, Production Company Scott Rudin Productions, Distributed by Paramount Pictures, June 1st, 1998, Los Angeles.

Mirror Mirror
"Mirror Mirror,"
Based on "Snow White" by the Brothers Grimm. Original work "Snow White and the Seven Dwarfs" Owners, Disney Enterprises, Inc., 1937.

Nightmare
"Never never land,"
Barrie, J.M., "Neverland." or "Peter Pan or The Boy Who Would Not Grow Up." 1911.

"Never never land,"
Hammett, Kirk, Hetfield, James, Ulrich, Lars, "Enter Sandman." Album "Metallica." Producers Bob, Rock, Hetfield, James, Ulrich, Lars. Studio One on One, July 29th, 1991, Los Angeles.

Intertwined
"Dr. Jekyll and Mr. Hyde,"
Stevenson, Robert Louis, "Strange Case of Dr. Jekyll and Mr. Hyde." Publisher Longman's Green and Co., January 5th 1886, United Kingdom.

Uneasy
"You hear the train a coming"
Cash, Johnny, "Folsom Prison Blues." Producer Johnston, Bob, Label Columbia, May 6th, 1968.

The Boogeyman
"Don't let me get me, I'm a hazard to myself."
Austin, Dallas, Pink. Produced by Austin, Dallas, Studio Pinetree Miami Beach, Florida, DARP, Atlanta, Georgia, Label Arista, BMG, February 18th, 2002.

"Black Swan"
Heinz, Andres. Screenplay by Heyman, Mark, Heinz, Andres, McLaughlin, John, Produced by Medavoy, Mike, Messer, Arnold W., Oliver, Brian, Franklin, Scott, Production Company Cross Creek Pictures, Protozoa Pictures, Phoenix Pictures, Dune Entertainment, Distributed by Fox Searchlight Pictures, December 3rd, 2010 (United States).

Protect
"chosen adventure"
Montgomery, R.A., Packard, Edward, and Stretch, Joe. "Choose Your Own Adventure." Publisher Bantam Books, 1979-1998.

Little Wound
"Pain, pain, go away, come again another day"
Wallace, Denslow Lia, "Rain, Rain, Go Away." from "Mother Goose." 1901. Nursery rhyme from 17th century or earlier.
Round, Steve. Round Folk Song Index number 19096.

Last Star
"Interstellar"
Nolan, Jonathan, Nolan, Christopher. "Interstellar." Produced by Thomas, Emma, Nolan, Christopher, Obst, Lynda, Produced by Paramount Pictures, Warner Bros. Pictures, Legendary Pictures, Syncopy Inc., Lynda Obst Productions, Distributed by Paramount Pictures (North America), Warner Bros. Pictures (International), November 4th, 2014 (United States).

Seas of Life
"seize the day"
Horace, "Book 1, 1.11", Odes, 23 B.C.

"Oh captain my captain"
Whitman, Walt, "Oh Captain! My Captain!" The Saturday Press, November 4th, 1865.

Walk Into Your Joy
"There's no place like home"
Baum, L. Frank, "The Wonderful Wizard of Oz." George L. Hill Company, May 17th, 1900.

"The Alchemist"
Coelho, Paulo, "O Alchemista." HarperTorch, 1988, in English 1993.

www.ingramcontent.com/pod-product-compliance
Lightning Source LLC
Chambersburg PA
CBHW052157220526
45471CB00004B/1702